The Last
Night

Anti-work, Atheism, Adventure

The Last Night

Night

Anti-work, Atheism, Adventure

Frederico Campagna

Winchester, UK
Washington, USA

First published by Zero Books, 2013
Zero Books is an imprint of John Hunt Publishing Ltd., Laurel House, Station Approach,
Alresford, Hants, SO24 9JH, UK
office1@jhpbooks.net
www.johnhuntpublishing.com
www.zero-books.net

For distributor details and how to order please visit the 'Ordering' section on our website.

Text copyright: Frederico Campagna 2013

ISBN: 978 1 78279 195 9

A CIP catalogue record for this book is available from the British Library.

Design: Stuart Davies

Printed and bound by CPI Group (UK) Ltd, Croydon, CR0 4YY

We operate a distinctive and ethical publishing philosophy in all
areas of our business, from our global network of authors to
production and worldwide distribution.

CONTENTS

This book was written for and is dedicated to teenagers.

Acknowledgements

I would like to thank Mark Fisher for commissioning and believing in this book, Franco Berardi Bifo for writing the introduction, and Saul Newman for writing the afterword. It's a real privilege to be surrounded by such inspiring thinkers and friends.

Special thanks to Lucy Mercer, who as well editing the book, has been an incredible support and intellectual counterpart throughout the writing process.

Thanks to my family, Luciano, Nellina and Elisabetta. Thanks also to all the many people that helped me develop the ideas and the style of the text, and in particular Anna Galkina, Henry Hartley, Alessio Kolioulis, Paolo Mossetti and Robert Prouse.

Thanks to Rowan Wilson at Verso Books for helping me to have the time to write this book, and thanks to Manlio Poltronieri for helping to maintain the online platform *Through Europe* where all the early stages of my work were published. And of course, thanks to everybody at the amazing Zero Books.

Architecture and war are not incompatible.
Architecture is war. War is architecture.
I am at war with my time, with history, with all authority
that resides in fixed and frightened forms.
I am one of millions who do not fit in, who have no home, no
    family,
no doctrine, no firm place to call my own, no known beginning
    or end,
no "sacred and primordial site."
I declare war on all icons and finalities, on all histories
that would chain me with my own falseness, my own pitiful fears.
I know only moments, and lifetimes that are as moments,
and forms that appear with infinite strength, then "melt into air."
I am an architect, a constructor of worlds,
a sensualist who worships the flesh, the melody,
a silhouette against the darkening sky.
I cannot know your name. Nor can you know mine.
Tomorrow, we begin together the construction of a city.
Lebbeus Woods, *War And Architecture*

Introduction

by Franco Berardi Bifo

Vanishing Modernity

The modern age was a time when human beings, alone or together, could sculpt the marble of history with the hammer of will. Today, both the marble of history and the hammer of will seem to have vanished from sight. There is no longer anything resembling the monumental vigour of intentional, conscious, organised action. More importantly, there is no longer a progressive temporal dimension, nor the possibility of reducing countless micro-changes to a prevailing tendency or a unitary temporality. Time has fragmented into an endless mosaic of schizo-instants, devoid of any continuity. In our perception, narrations and production, time has become fractalised, shattering into compatible splinters of time constantly re-combined and put to work by the universal linguistic machine. Communication is increasingly (and almost exclusively) a frantic connection mediated by electronic screens. Work is relentless shifting between the nodes of the metropolis or of the planet. Words have lost their carnal texture and the trajectories of work meet each other instantly only in order to diverge and re-connect, never meeting each other again.

A precarious culture is emerging from the horizon of our time, and this book is a presage of the tide to come.

I have lived through the tail end of the modern experience. I witnessed the vanishing of modernity, I underwent it and I tried to interpret it. Thus, I read Federico Campagna's work as a map of the shifts (often microscopic, barely perceptible) of sensibility from the sphere of modernity to that of precarity. Because, –

beware – precarity is not a provisional, transient, resolvable juncture of social and productive relations. Precarity is the time that comes after modernity.

The Precarious Horizon

What is the precarious condition? It is not simply the condition of millions of people who work without a permanent contract or without any guarantee of what will happen to their salary the following day. It is the condition in which every night is the last night, awakening from which each one of us sinks into the carriage of an underground train in order to perform their solitary, hyper-connected journey.

The question we are asking ourselves today is: what stage of the night is it?

And somebody comes to warn us that this is the night that does not end. What stage of the night is this? Is this perhaps the point in which we realise that the night is not ending?

Modernity concerned itself with building shelters, protections, guarantees, so it could push back the spectre of death. But now that the tempest has blown away our shelters, we begin to realise that the weak secularism of the modern age has only managed to put death between brackets. We have not learnt how to talk about death, and now death looks at us, contemptuous and sneering, from every corner of the social life. The precarious condition is naked against the cold, winds, hunger, violence. Precarity is bare life as exposed to the truth of death. There is no return from the precarious condition, because it reveals a truth that for too long we have been hiding from ourselves, and of which we are now finally aware.

Death inscribes itself within the horizon of radical, autonomous, materialist thinking, because it is only by knowing the limit of our time and of our lives that we might be able to understand that which dialectic (idealist) communism has stopped us from seeing: that the winner wins nothing, and that the struggle for freedom is doomed to failure from the start. And that only in an aware state of autonomy from the awareness of the inevitable it is possible to live happily, and to die consciously, that is – freely.

Radical atheism begins again from scratch, looking at existence from the point of view of death.

Is this the sign of a political defeat?

Or is it perhaps the beginning of a precarious humanism, looking for a happy harmony with chaos?

Us

The emerging precarious culture manifests itself in an existence, aesthetics, literary and artistic production that is marked by the quest for 'us'.

I took part in the political movements of the past few decades, the huge gatherings of waving, raging and tender bodies, but I never thought that I was fighting for an idea. I was fighting for us.

I was fighting for my friends, millions of friends whom I knew because I knew that they were struggling, as I was, to live a life that was freed from sadness, exploitation and violence.

It was easy for the modern generations to say 'us', for those working in the factories, for the intellectuals crowding the meetings of the artistic and political vanguards of the 20th Century, brightened by electric lights. Singular existences used to recompose easily and almost naturally in a mix of bodies and words that allowed the formation of a shared flow of sociality and experience – more than a common belonging or identity. Solidarity was the political (and admittedly a bit rhetorical) word that used to convey this immediate experience of being together, sharing the same path, the same interests and the same destiny.

But what is the precarious 'us', how is the precarious tissue of the experience of 'us' made?

Precariousness of the collective perception is the anguish of failing to find each other, while endlessly, frantically meeting each other along the paths of connection.

Event, singularity, desire – these words, which Federico Campagna melts into the word 'adventure', look for a plane of existential commonality after the loss of the permanent immediacy of 'us'. The precarious 'us' goes looking for itself along the narrow, dangerous trails of adventure, which don't allow many to pass together, but only one at a time in single file.

1

Migrating

Imagine growing up as a young atheist in a stiflingly Catholic country.

Imagine migrating to London, the Babylon of 'really existing atheism'.

Imagine the expectations.

When I first set foot on the cold, secular ground of the metropolis, I felt that I couldn't have asked for more. A few empty churches, scattered here and there. No Vatican City, no Pope. Charles Darwin's face on banknotes. I could finally breathe freely.

Yet I realised quickly that something wasn't right. Somehow, the smell of religion still lingered in the air, as sickening as always. I found it on the trains coming back home from the office, filled with exhausted workers. I smelt it on the benches on a Monday afternoon, covered with the beer cans of the unemployed. Most of all, I felt it surrounding me when I walked into the office every morning, finding my colleagues already there, frantically typing on their keyboards as if fiddling with digital rosaries. I had walked in perfectly on time, why was everybody there already? Why did they look so satisfied when they greeted me from their desks? They were working hard, harder than they were expected to. And in the evening, when the darkness of Northern Europe enveloped the office blocks and young professionals' houses, they were still at their desks, typing as fast as greyhounds race. Looking at me packing up, as if I had been a weak opponent abandoning the match before time. Why did they keep working late, when no pay or praise was ever to be awarded to them by anybody? What did they find in their silent, tragic sacrifice?

Once again I was surrounded by that smell. The same smell that filled the churches of my childhood on a Sunday morning. It had spread everywhere. Not just in churches, but all around the office blocks. Not just confined to one day a week, but every day – eight, nine ten hours a day. No longer accompanied by the chanting of monks, but by the clicking march of a million ants on the keyboard of one, immense metropolitan organ.

Religion had never left. I had never managed to escape it. Its name had changed, but its believers remained the same. They were just a little more honest, a little more self-sacrificing than the old Catholics back at home. Possibly, a little more fanatical.

Radical Atheism

A New Faith

At the beginning of the 21st Century, Westerners seemed to have reached the stage in which their aspirations to autonomy and freedom could finally become reality.

After centuries of secularism, traditional religions appeared to have lost their hypnotic powers. Together with the emptying of churches, the cult of the 'true gods' had shrunk into the object of purely academic research, or a handle for the desperate clinging of the most impoverished masses. At the same time, the blood-baths of the 20th Century's total wars, betrayed revolutions and political nightmares had managed to break the spell of even the most insidious secular religions. Fascism had lost any rights of citizenship within the political discourse. Communism had turned into the pet-idea of intellectually oriented art institutions, the earthly limbo of failed utopias. Capitalism's pretence of being the only possible, rational global system had shattered against its own contradictions. As everything tilted on the verge of an epochal change, the notion of time opened itself to transformation. The linear progression of past, present and future had ceased to act as the herdsman of human populations, no longer pushing them towards the epic massacres that always accompany idealistic delusions. Historical time seemed to have vanished, clearing the sky above everyday life. And together with the end of History, the bundle of promises of Progress had also finally run out of string.

In front of Westerners, the future opened like an unmapped oceanic expanse, emerging through the cracks of the earth. No routes were set for them to sail along obediently. Admirals and priests relinquished their position, claiming to have always been simply part of the crew. Flags were taken down the masts and set alight. The laces holding abstract social morality on Westerners' heads, like the incandescent helmets used in medieval torture, were loosened. At last, they could swap the ill-fated demand for freedom *of* religion with the emancipatory cry for freedom *from* any religion. At last, they could build for themselves communities that did not irradiate from any central totem. No longer would they have to seek the autonomy of capital, of knowledge or of the law above them, but they could assert their own autonomy above any abstraction.

But none of this happened. When the religious mist above their heads vanished, and they saw that the stars were nothing but cold lights indifferent to their fate, panic overwhelmed them. The limit between freedom and despair suddenly turned too thin. Unshielded by religion or ideology, the horizon appeared to them as too wide, and the wind too strong. How could a person know how to behave, if no God told them what to do? The nervous systems of the Westerners cracked, letting them sink into a self-harming frenzy. They needed a new, low roof above their head. They needed a new form of reassurance.

As inspired by panic, their plan for engineering their own, new submission neared a perverse logical perfection. They knew that if they built another idol to rule over them, another God of sorts, or ideology, they would have to spend their nights in fear of yet another catastrophic collapse of their faith. Gods rise and fall, ideologies crumble, on battlefields as well as on the stock market. Even golden calves can be melted and turned into earrings. They also realised that prayers were not the tools to employ in their dealings with superior powers, since their prayers had never managed to maintain the kingdoms of their defunct Gods.

What they needed was a new, self-fulfilling type of prayer, which was not directed at any Gods that could betray them.

In fact, what they really needed wasn't a prayer, but a mantra: an invocation that revolves on itself, a spell that endlessly produces itself, a belief in believing.

Yet, in its traditional form, a mantra is too impractical a routine to be of any use to others than monks and hermits. If they ever wanted to apply it to their everyday life, Westerners had to find a way of adapting this mystical exercise to the structures of contemporary capitalism. What would a mantra look like, in the heart of a global metropolis of the 21st Century? What other act might be able to host its obsessive spirit, whilst functioning like a round, magic shield, covering the frightened believers from their fear of freedom?

There was only one possible, almost perfect candidate. The activity of repetition *par excellence*: Work. The endless chain of gestures and movements that had built the pyramids and dug the mass graves of the past. The seal of a new alliance with all that is divine, which would be able to bind once again the whole of humanity to a new and eternal submission. The act of submission to submission itself.

Work.

The new, true faith of the future.

The Paradox of Work

What do we talk about, when we talk about Work?

Clearly, we talk about the type of activity that produces all the artefacts we see around us. Work is the origin of the pipe and the wall, of milk and bread, of smiling customer service, of police, of the plumber and the washing machine. But we would be mistaken, if we thought that such products and services are the main *raison d'être* for Work, today. Products and services are only its most spectacular outcome, but no longer its core aim. It is simpler to understand this distinction if we look back at traditional conscription armies. On a superficial level, it might seem reasonable to believe that their belligerent outcome was the main, if not the only, object of their production. Supposedly armies were only a means to war. Yet, that was hardly the case. War was the most spectacular outcome of traditional armies, but not the main focus of their production. Above all else, armies produced discipline, both in peace and in wartime.

Similarly, products and services constitute Work's most spectacular outcome, but in the present day they can hardly be considered as its core production.

This disjunction between Work and economic production becomes especially clear if we consider the economic paradox that characterises contemporary Work.

On the one hand, we have a global economy that is cyclically devastated by recurrent crises of overproduction. The endless supply that pours out of our factories and offices under the dogma of limitless economic growth, does not meet an equivalent level of demand, as should be the case in a capitalist economy. Every so many years, a crisis or a war is needed in order to destroy the supply in excess. We produce too much, we Work too much, and by doing so we regularly destroy our economy. An even more dramatic state of affairs belongs to the relationship between production and the natural environment. In order to fuel current levels of overproduction – as well as overconsumption, although only in terms of industrial, rather than individual consumption – we are progressively and stubbornly devastating the collection of natural resources which goes under the name of 'the environment'. Overproduction does not only destroy the global economy, but the global biosphere. Our excessive Work not only leads to economic crisis, but to an environmental catastrophe. Finally, we now have at our disposal a set of technologies that would be able to make most of human labour redundant. Instead of profiting from the ease allowed by a production devolved to machines, humans find themselves competing against technology and are thus forced to reduce their demands and expectations to the level of the machine. We try to work as much and as tirelessly as machines do, and by doing so we turn ourselves into second-rate production machines, never as efficient as the real ones.

On the other hand, the discourse over Work is now more obsessive then ever. For the vast majority of the world population waged-labour still remains the only possible way of accessing the resources necessary for survival. Especially in the West, the army of the tragically overworked – fed on psychoactive drugs and self-help remedies – faces the hordes of the equally tragically unemployed. Work does not simply act as the only entrance to the market of resources, but also as the main platform for the exchange of social recognition, and as the intimate theatre of happiness. It is not only in front of their peers, but also in front of themselves, that a person's worth is defined by their job and by their level of productivity. Every moment of the day that escapes the universe of Work is a wasted moment, a time of despair and loneliness. Without Work, outside of Work, we are nothing, and so much so that even consumption has had to be turned into a Work-related activity. The office has become the place where we are supposed to find our happiness and self-respect – or, to say it in the new-age parlance of office culture, to 'find ourselves' – as well as the love of what we do: is there any place where we can feel safer than when we are in our workplace, snug in the warm embrace of our office family?

I define this as an economic paradox, since the signals given by economic and environmental devastation, combined with the availability of labour-reducing technologies, logically point towards a dramatic downsizing of human investment into Work. Yet, as we have seen, the cultural discourse around Work seems to be speeding in the opposite direction, claiming an ever-greater role for it in our lives and in the construction of our economic, social and even affective environment.

How is this possible? If the effects of contemporary Work are both unnecessary and harmful, why do we continue investing everything in it? What is Work for?

A History of Obedience

Traditional conscription armies produced discipline, the most precious resource for traditional, *ancien régime* societies. Contemporary offices and factories produce obedience, the necessary cement for a society struggling to maintain an abstract, immortal roof over its head. If we want to understand this relationship between obedience and Religion, we must begin by taking a closer look at obedience itself.

There is often a deep misunderstanding about the relationship between power and obedience. We are used to believing that obedience is submitted to the power that rules over it, both in a logical and a productive sense. We are used to considering the command of the master as productive of the activity of those submitted to it. We couldn't be more mistaken. Without the obedience of the slave, the orders of the masters would be little more than barks in the wind. Even when displayed with the outmost authority and supported by the most brutal force, power could do nothing without obedience. It is the obedience of the worker that replenishes the storages of the master, which polishes the master's silverware and protects his home. The relationship between power and obedience is the same as that between capital and labour: if capital is nothing but crystallised labour – which collapses as a coercive reality over the labourers themselves – then power is nothing but crystallised obedience, which collapses like an avalanche over the very heads of those who obey. Power is powerless, obedience is all-powerful.

After such considerations, a question arises almost spontaneously: if power is so weak, to the point of being unable to exist without the active obedience of those who submit to it, then why do people obey? Who do we obey? Clearly, nobody would ever do anything if they did not think that it would bring them some advantage of some type. Nobody would obey for the sake of it, but always as a means to an end. Yet, we should not look for these ends in the catalogue of immediately material benefits, but rather in what we defined before as the realm of Religion.

A look at the history of obedience could help us to clarify such a utilitarian reading of the relationship between obedience and Religion.

When we talk about the history of obedience, we could as well invert the order of the words and talk about the obedience of History. History and obedience have always, and by necessity, travelled together, since their common origin in the invention of writing. According to traditional historiography, we can define as History the period of time that begins with the first appearance of written records 3,200 years BC. Such written records, as discovered by archaeologists in the area anciently known as Mesopotamia, were the clay tablets issued by the temples in their dealing with the local peasant population. At that time, Mesopotamian temples used to function both as places of worship and as storages for the seeds and tools used for agriculture. Temples used to lend seeds and tools to peasants, and recorded the peasants' debts on the tablets. If a peasant was unable to repay his debt, both him and his family would have to pay back with their own freedom. It was a custom that every new king would destroy all the tablets at the beginning of their kingdom or at the end of a successful war campaign. But the temple's cunning accountants soon found a way around the inconvenience of royal mercy. Together with the first form of writing and of debt, the first clause was invented: the temple accountants began to insert a non-termination clause to all their new debt tablets. The debt was to be active forever, regardless of the decisions of the king.

The effects of the invention of this clause were tremendous, far exceeding the grey world of mere accountancy. We could say that with the immortalisation of peasants' debts through writing, the very composition of the world changed. Until that moment, all that existed were living creatures, floating over the thin layer of mortality, and lifeless, inorganic matter. Even the immortality of the gods was rather relative, and often more akin to the mortal fragility of humans than to the celestial serenity typical of the gods of monotheistic religions. With the introduction of the non-termination clause, for the first time abstract immortality appeared. Something consciously created by humans suddenly rose above their heads and began a life of its own: a life that could potentially transcend and survive that of its creators. First debts, then laws, then History itself: the flesh became word, and its abstract, immortal form fell again over the living, crushing them, binding them hand and foot. This man-made space of immortality – which we could define as a space of 'normative abstraction' – wrapped itself around human lives as their second nature. Alongside biological nature, which limited and defined the sphere of human action and possibility, the second nature of normative abstractions cut an even stricter, narrower border. Humans had created it, yet they could not undo it. While people died, the written word was immortal and its commands were to be perennially productive. Civilisation was born. With the realisation of their powerlessness, humans first experienced panic, then fear and finally, envy. They started to desire immortality for themselves. They wanted to acquire it or, better, they wanted to be allowed within its immortal fields.

How to become immortal? How to gain a seat in the choir of abstractions? This is the fundamental question at the heart of most religions, and the point at which the religious strategies of theologians and those of 'common' believers seem to diverge the most. While theologians often propose the philosophical contemplation of pure forms or of the divine essence as a solution to the quest for immortality, the vast majority of believers traditionally lean towards two different sets of answers.

On the one hand, we have the typically Christian work on the body, as epitomised by the ritual of communion. In order to be allowed into the space of immortality, believers have to begin by transforming their bodies. Ingesting the 'body of Christ', however, is not enough, as the flesh needs to be tormented, humiliated and deprived of enjoyment, so that it may become of the same bloodless matter of the abstraction.

On the other hand, there is the method of Islam that is, literally in Arabic, of 'submission'. The measure of one's ability to perform submission becomes the currency that would ultimately buy the believer their ticket to the abstract fields of immortality. Submission to the immortal, normative abstraction has to be complete, visible in deed and embodied in the everyday practice of human life. Here Islam meets Protestant ethics, the ritual of prayers meets the routine of factory and office work, and the fanaticism of traditional religion meets that of modern unreligions. It is only by surrendering our will to the abstraction that we, worthless, mortal flesh, might one day be allowed to become as immortal as the abstractions that we erected over our heads. It is by working harder, by turning ourselves into machines, that we will be able to turn our flesh into the steel that built our chains. Becoming the chain takes the place of the desire to break away from it.

Finance of Immortality

Has anyone ever managed to become immortal?

Some have achieved the immortality of the Unknown Soldier, with the remnants of their flesh mixed with those of other devastated bodies, locked within a monument in a Capital City square. Others have joined the graveyard of dead writers, having their name engraved on the spine of a book, together with all the other paper tombstones lined on the grids of a library's bookshelves. None of them, however, really made it. Mortals are dying creatures, without redemption. Life as such is a mechanism, which contains in itself its own negation and its own constant sabotage.

So, why do we keep trying? Why over the last five thousand years have men and women destroyed each others' lives and – most often – destroyed their own life, in the name of an immortality that they could never achieve?

Possibly, the reason for such a bad 'investment' is to be found in the financial characteristics of the dealing between humans and immortal, normative abstractions. The transaction taking place between them is not of the common, direct type. It refers more to the financial system than to the everyday economy of the grocery shop. We can observe it under the lens of basic finance: lending and borrowing. Differently from the times of the Mesopotamian temples, positions here have swapped, as we have the individual workers as the creditors, and normative abstractions and their temples as debtors. Obedient believers lend their energy and life-time to their normative abstraction of choice – the Nation, a Career, God, Progress, etc – as they work hard to maintain its abstract, immortal kingdom. Seen from the other perspective, we may say that a normative abstraction opens a line of debt on its believers' lives, from which it extracts all the necessary sacrifice and obedience that it needs in order to consolidate its kingdom. In return, the normative abstraction provides its creditors with a system of repayment, which unfolds along two parallel levels.

On the one level, it repays what we may define as the 'interests' on its debt through the monetary transactions typical of wage-labour. Although we are used to believing that monetary salary is the full repayment of the life-time that we lend to those we work for, the truth is that money can only possibly repay the interests on our lending. If it were to be repaid in its core, in fact, a credit of life-time would need to be repaid with an equivalent amount of life-time – which is clearly impossible.

On the other level, in order to repay the core of its debt through some sort of currency equivalent to life-time, the normative abstraction adopts the system of the promise. Since life cannot be added to life, and workers and believers cannot be made to live longer in the flesh, their repayment is postponed indefinitely. Their obedience will be repaid through an immortality, which will happen after life. Although the concept of heavenly afterlife is more explicitly stated in traditional religions, contemporary secular faiths still maintain it, though in a more subtle form. For most of us, workers under Capitalism, this rupture with the life of the flesh is sanctioned by the arrival of Success in our Career. According to capitalist rhetoric, Success, like Revolution, is a moment in which everything changes: nothing will be the same again, not even the flesh, reincarnated in the expensive clothes of the successful businessman or woman. While most tabloid celebrities represent only the pagan embodiment of success – re-enacting a set of tragicomic interactions worthy of the squabbles among Greek gods – other characters, such as Steve Jobs or Bill Gates, incarnate the perfect capitalist equivalent of a Catholic Saint. They used to be common mortals like us, until Success – like a happy martyrdom – transcended their bodies into the thin air of the Ideal.

But a promise is not enough, unless it comes with an immediate, tangible complement. Humans are greedy creatures, and they need something to hold in their avid hands. The system of the promise, as deployed by normative abstractions, does not come without this necessary complement. Although its means of payment is not monetary, the currency which it employs is not that dissimilar in its functioning to contemporary money: hope.

A promise, in the course of its action and until the moment of its deliverance, generously pours an abundant stock of hope into the hands of the believer. Hope is given by a normative abstraction to its creditors as a guarantee of repayment of its core debt – which will only take place after the death of the flesh. The specific relationship that this transaction creates between debtor and lender puts in place the same paradoxical, dangerous coincidence of interests that exists between moneylenders and money creditors. As we know, current account holders are the largest moneylenders in today's world, alongside whom banks act as the largest borrowers of money. If every single account holder was to withdraw his or her stock of money lent to their bank, they would soon bring the entire bank system to collapse and, in doing so, they would bring their own stock of money to a near-zero value. Money lent to banks cannot be retrieved in full, ever. Similarly, hope can never be fully claimed back, unless the creditor – that is, the obedient worker – wants to see his or her stock of hope be devalued to nothing, as the system of the promise crumbles. The believer in the capitalist abstraction of a Career cannot afford to claim back his or her stock of hope in full. Career would not deliver its promise of Success, and all the years spent in hard work and sacrifices would cease to exist even in the virtual currency of hope, so similar in this respect to the virtual currency of contemporary money. In the same way, the believer in the abstraction of Revolution can never demand to withdraw in full their stock of hope. Revolution will not happen today – maybe tomorrow, always tomorrow – and even if it did, it would not be a good thing: what would be left to the believer, if their dream was to be realised once and for all? What would remain to the revolutionary worker, if the Revolution was to happen? Maybe a place in some politburo, below a picture of the great leader, but nothing compares to the immense, overflowing, ultimately useless stock of hope accumulated in a lifetime of obedience.

Radical Atheism

Let us recap.

We began by talking about religion. Although its traditional mask has vanished from sight, what has been revealed underneath is the steel-hard structure of its essence. The idols and gods of the past have vacated their throne, but the throne still remains. Afraid of the possibility of their autonomy – if we don't dare to say freedom – humans elected their very submission to the throne as their new God. A truly invincible, invisible God. Within the landscape of contemporary life, such submission takes place in the form of Work, and in particular of a kind of Work that no longer retains any believable relation to economic production.

Since the beginning of History and Civilisation, humans have worshipped normative abstractions, and in particular the space of immortality in which they exist. Their worshipping, of course, was not dictated by love and admiration, but by a resentful feeling of envy. Humans wanted to gain access to that space of immortality, and submitting completely to those who lived in it – the Gods – seemed to be the best way of achieving their goal. In this sense, a type of activity which is striking for its unproductiveness and absurdity – such as Work today – functioned as the perfect tool, possibly the most minimal and most effective. Yet, their desires were never to be repaid. Nobody ever gained true immortality, and all of them died cursing their wasted lives. The only reason why they continued – and they have been doing so for almost five millennia – was their acceptance of the debt-notes issued by normative abstractions, that is, of their promises with their complement of hope.

And so we have a picture of the believer today: the contemporary worker. Somebody endlessly sailing towards a receding horizon, while their ship is sinking under the burden of a ton of worthless credit notes.

We thought Religion had vanished, but in fact it had concentrated its strength and expanded its size, ramifying so tightly around human activities that the ivy of abstraction is hardly distinguishable from the roots of our nerves. It did it so blatantly that at first we did not realise it. Any project of disentanglement from the Religious loop must begin by acknowledging the immensity of the task. Thus, if we ever wanted to embark on such a project, we should understand our attempt as that of creating a truly radical atheism.

A method of radical atheism has to be universal in its scope, in that it aims at the full disentanglement of our existential world from any religious mantra, yet it should not be such in its reach. Reducing it to an object of propaganda would not only be a horrible aberration, but would also be unnecessary, since radical atheism cannot become another ecumenical faith requiring the universal agreement (or annihilation) of all members of Humanity in order to take place. Religious believers will always continue to exist, regardless of our efforts or our desires, and they will probably remain the majority of the flesh existing on this planet. Radical atheism should simply be a tool for those who desire to exit the systems of Promise and Religion, and to escape from the seductive grip of their chains.

In defining radical atheism, it is also important to notice how its aim should not be that of presenting itself to the razor-sharp eyes of academic scrutiny as a perfectly polished, perfectly spherical hard bone of ideological and theoretical consistency. The only scrutiny that it should undergo – as a method of existential liberation – is that of individual utility and effectiveness in regards to its goals. And its main goal is the production of autonomy and the creation of the conditions for an individual to take control over his or her life and to enjoy this life fully and within its limits.

Mentioning the importance of limits in what almost sounds like a radical manifesto is certainly an unusual move, which invokes the oft-disdained smell of compromises and calls to order. Yet, it is exactly from the understanding of the limits of our lives and of our enjoyment of them, that radical atheism can begin its action. Religion, in all its forms, typically unfolds along a trajectory that transcends the limited temporality of mortal lives, towards the immortal horizon of abstractions. Radical atheism operates exactly outside of that horizon, and only within the limits of a mortal life. In front of the mauled body of the soldier scattered on the battlefield, Religion sees the potential for immortality in the abstract fields of History. Radical atheism only sees the explosion of the limits of his flesh. In the face of the customary overtime of most workers, Religion sees the expansion of the limits of their mortality, stretching towards the abstract shores of Success. Radical atheism only sees the inhibition of enjoyment within a life that demanded too much from itself. If Religion looks at death as a new beginning, radical atheism sees it as the ultimate end: not only the end of one's world, but the end of the whole world, the end of everything. If Religion – especially in its contemporary, capitalist declination – sees resources as endlessly renewable, radical atheism understands everything as mortal and hopelessly limited.

Radical atheism operates as the simultaneous acknowledgement of the smallness of individual mortal lives, and of the immensity of their hunger. Its method can be described as the art of eating, while we still have a mouth to eat with, and to eat as mortals, within the limits of our stomach and of our appetite. It is the process of destroying our cultural 'second nature', while exploring the space of our biological nature to its limits – or to the limits of our desire to do so.

2

The Last Night

One night, not too long ago, I found myself lying on a hospital bed, saturated with morphine. I wasn't sure what exactly was happening to me, but I knew it wasn't good. The doctor kept walking in and out of the room, nervously checking my X-rays. He wouldn't talk to me, and the nurse stuck to professional silence. Something was happening. It was happening to me. Was that it? Was it the end?

I used to believe the myth that upon one's death, one was entitled to the short, condensed film of an entire lifetime flashing before one's eyes. So I waited for the screening to begin on the cloudy surface of my morphined eyelids. But no visual recollection appeared to give me my share of cinematic existentialism. There were no images of my first girlfriend to bring a tear to my eyes, nor the slow-motion re-enactment of a long-forgotten hug with my father. I felt no nostalgia, no inner peace. There was only a sharp feeling of anger, ripping its way through the layers of sedatives.

Anger for the hours I spent at school, when I was a child. Anger for the morning sleepiness on the trains to work, while my life melted in a blur alongside that of all the other commuters. Anger for the summer days spent in the office, for the late shifts at work, for the cocktail parties, for the enforced fun. Anger for all I didn't do, in the name of something that now was nowhere near to give me my pay back. Anger towards myself, for my unforgivable obedience. Why had I wasted so much of my life trying to believe in the 'higher purpose' of what I was doing? Why had I blindly poured so much of my energies in my studies, in my career, in my good behaviour, if everything was now coming to an end, with no possibility of return?

Clearly, in the end, I didn't die. The doctor came back, said something about an operation and stuck a tube into my chest. It wasn't that bad, after all. I admit it, I was being a little melodramatic. Yet, the feelings and the anger that had possessed me were true: I had really thought that I was going to die.

In the days that followed, the thought of my coming encounter with another such moment took hold of me completely. I didn't want it to be like that again. I didn't want to see myself aged, lying on a hospital bed, once again sedated, shivering for the anger of having wasted so many years, so many more then those I have wasted so far. If all the promises of the abstractions I have believed in have revealed themselves as utterly vacuous – if not as complete scams – the urgency of those thoughts were still vivid in front of me in their honest reality. Revolution might never happen, Progress might be just a line traced in the sand, Success a carrot at the end of a stick, but that anger, that desperate feeling of having wasted the little, precious time I had, was real, and it urged me to take action.

Squandering

An Antidote

For too long Religion has been compared to opium. Opium slows down physical and cognitive processes, invites the smoker or eater to close their eyes, to take a rest. Opium lies over life like a mosquito net, keeping all the noise of the world at bay, freezing life in a permanent dawn. Religion doesn't work this way, neither in the traditional religion of the Holy Church, nor in its secular, contemporary versions. Religion enters the bloodstream and pushes the heartbeat beyond its limits. It sets the neural paths on fire, then collides thoughts against the muscular tissue, until the bloodshed is abundant enough to fuel an obsessive hyperactivity, which escapes human reason and possibilities. It might resemble amphetamine more than opium, crystal meth even more than amphetamine. Most of all, it functions like a poison. A substance which does not cover life like a light blanket, but which enters it like a raping agent, distorting it, taking it over, burning it until it is no more: overwork, self-sacrifice, crusades, the megalomania of suicide cases in the name of one normative abstraction or another.

If Religion is a poison, does it come without an antidote? Some might be tempted to draw from the Greek word for poison, *pharmakos*, which had 'medicine' as its second meaning, thus understanding poison and antidote as two aspects of the same nature. Along this path of reasoning, they might be inclined to believe that inoculating the patient with a moderate amount of the aggressive agent, as in the method of vaccination, may function as an effective cure. They will advocate that a better, wiser, more considerate use of Religion might be the appropriate vaccination against its excessive use: moderate patriotism to fight

Nationalism, secular Islam to combat Muslim fundamentalism, strict work regulations to avoid overexploitation, and so on. Although some of these proposals might have some positive effects on the short-term, they hardly succeed in neutralising the power and ambition of Religion. Vaccination acts well against viruses, fellow living creatures which parasite the human host from within. But Religion, like poison, is only alive as a metaphor, and it does not share the same plane of existence with the veins it penetrates and corrodes. We don't need a vaccination to Religion, we need an antidote: an agent that acts in the opposite direction of the poison, with its same strength.

This negative, frontal opposition between the poison and its antidote allows us to restrict the field of our research. If religious discourses originate from the immortal sphere of normative abstractions, the antidote that we are seeking must exist outside of this sphere. It will only be found and will only function within the limits of the mortal life of the flesh. If the poison of Religion imposes itself on us like the totalising view of a horizon, always out of arm's reach, always within the illusory grasp of the eye, then its antidote, like a tool, must have a handle for us to use it. It will not be another normative abstraction, but a method of action.

Have humans ever encountered such a prodigious tool, or is it just another mythological invention? We have lived alongside it for a very long time, possibly as long as we have lived under the shadow of religious thinking. We have even invented a word for it. Unsurprisingly, it is a word with a strong, pejorative connotation. Its Latin version, *dilapidatio*, derived semantically from the act of pelting with stones – possibly both in the sense of its destructive effects and in that of the supposedly deserved punishment for those who enacted it. More recently, its contemporary name is often to be found in the reproaches of concerned parents, or in the tearful indignation of professional politicians in times of crisis. 'Squandering' is the English word under which our antidote has been hidden for centuries, and this is the name that we can still use today to define it.

Squandering, what a dangerous word. So much so that we have long learnt to pin it down, putting it under the tight guard of more reassuring practices. Many have put the practice of potlatch at its side as a stone guardian, in the hope that its mitigating effects might weaken the power of the captive. During potlatch, members of a community destroy or freely distribute a consistent part of their wealth, in order to demonstrate their social status and to reaffirm their bonds with their community. Despite appearances, potlatch still remains a highly religious gesture. The sacrifice of wealth that is performed in its name might not be directed towards the totem of any traditional god, but it is certainly aimed at conquering the favour of a social divinity. Its linear direction is from within the individual, all the way towards the ideal of a perfect unity of the Community, and towards the recognition of one's status within it. Squandering, on the contrary, unfolds along the trajectory of a boomerang. Squanderers dissipate their own wealth, but they do so only in their own interest and for their own enjoyment. Within the act of squandering there is no room for the abstraction of the Community, nor for the closed, metallic unity of the social body, which so intimately resembles that of a Nuremberg Virgin.

On the other side of squandering, centuries of Western tradition have erected the gigantic steel guardian of renunciation. Its features are the same as the smooth-cheeked face of young Saint Francis of Assisi, who on a long-past day in April stripped himself naked of his expensive clothes in front of the whole town, renouncing all his material possessions and his social status. Whilst at a first glance such an act might look similar to squandering, it was in fact imbued with the essence of Religion. His renunciation of the wealth of his family was a huge, swift exchange of material goods for the immaterial stock of the religious promise. His abandonment of the local community of Assisi was the process through which he could gain entrance to the real, perfect, immortal community of the choir gathered around God's throne.

Disrespectful Opportunism

Examples of the squandering method abound all around us. However, there is one that is particularly dear to me, perhaps for purely sentimental reasons, since I'm from the same Mediterranean island where such squandering once took place. The example I'm thinking of is the tragic parable of Sicilian aristocracy. Sicilian noblemen provide one of the finest and most effective examples of this method in practice, possibly only challenged by their counterparts in Russia. So committed were they to their squandering, that they managed to self-destruct as a class decades before the official abolition of the Italian aristocratic orders in 1945. Not a small achievement, if their self-annihilation is compared with the fate of their British equivalents, who are still firmly seated on the saddle of their society. Indeed, it was a matter of fate: in Latin, *fortuna*. Upon squandering their family inheritance, their fortune, Sicilian aristocrats didn't only dissipate their worldly possessions. They squandered their fate, drunkenly burning it together with their family mansions and dancing on its charred ruins. What at first seemed little more than a lustful mismanagement of their resources, was in fact a straight line pointed towards social suicide. Their behaviour wasn't simply the crapulousness of posh kids, or the squalid nightly impulses of contemporary bankers. They squandered their fortunes with such commitment and to such an extent, that they made it impossible for themselves to ever rely on the safety net of the system of the promise of their social class.

They didn't only lose their wealth, but their status and their honour. Their behaviour was shameful – though never ashamed of itself – and it made them unworthy of reproducing the aristocratic order. Their promise was broken. Their hope, squandered. We could say that they stuffed their faces with delicacies and scarred them with syphilis, so to make them too deformed to ever again wear the standard mask of the aristocrat. Their sexuality knew no purpose or boundaries: it was pornographic sterility, with no heir to pick up the thread and rebuild the ruins of their family mansions. They lost all respect towards the abstract promises of the aristocratic order, and by doing so they lost all the respect that was due to them as aristocrats.

We should linger for a moment over this word, 'respect'. Its origin is the Latin word *respicere*, which literally means 'to look back at' something. According to this etymology, to be respectful towards a system of belief thus presupposes a mirror-effect attached to every object: as one looks at a possible action or resource, one's gaze is mirrored back, 'looking back towards' the founding religious promise which one has bought into. This act of looking backwards is the very gesture through which one loads one's actions and possessions with the hopes and hidden meanings typical of the religious promise. Respect is the inner smith that constantly forges one's own religious chains. By adopting the method of squandering, Sicilian aristocrats chose not to 'look back at' the promises of their order. In fact, they looked away. Whenever their stare lighted upon an object or on the possibility of an action, what they saw was no longer the optical illusion of hope – the promise of moving one step further towards the mystical marriage with the immortality of abstractions – but simply the limited shape of a container full of opportunities for enjoyment. They no longer considered the world around them as an immortal catalogue of different degrees of perfection and truth, but as a mortal, blooming orchard of opportunities. They were disrespectful, and opportunists. Squanderers always are, by necessity, disrespectful opportunists. They have no honour, no belonging, no shame. Their world is populated by possibilities, and it is confined only by the limits of one's biological nature, of one's appetite and reason. As they close their eyes to the deceiving spectacles of immortality, they experience the world almost tactilely, on the tip of their tongue.

Perfect Criminals

One might object that it was easy for Sicilian aristocrats to squander their fortunes, ending their lifetimes with their safes still overflowing with treasures. But if we were to squander our possessions, would it take us longer than a couple of days of mindless dissipation? If we are to become squanderers, do we have to condemn ourselves to utter poverty?

Let us be clear on this: squandering, disrespectful opportunism and radical atheism are not a new declination of punk ethics. Squandering shares with punk the same despise for social, moral and ultimately religious institutions. Yet, in contrast, it does not present itself as a negative answer to them. If punk rejects any object or behaviour that was ever touched by Religion – however enjoyable or useful it might be – squanderers (that is, radical atheists and disrespectful opportunists) do not deny themselves *a priori* the possibility of enjoying those resources that are available to them. Punks are self-destructive monks, and their dirty hair and devastated arms are the same as those of Symeon the Stylite, the ancient Christian ascetic who lived on top of a pillar, pointing his arms towards the sky in an attempt to desiccate them for the glory of the Lord. Punks are honourable, they are consistent and uncompromising: they serve their Ideal, which is only a negative copy of the 'decent' bourgeois ideal. Like the Satanists, they are priests in disguise.

Equally, squandering has nothing to do with any contemporary, hippy-esque version of pauperism. Like pauperists, squanderers do not believe in the promises of social status and socially legitimated wealth. However, unlike pauperists, they do not deny the possible advantages that might come from the possession and the use/abuse of resource-wealth. The pauperist's viewpoint is that of an entity without a stomach, a being which already lives as if in the immortal world of abstractions. Pauperists, even in their contemporary, neoprimitivist incarnations, mistake the prefiguration of autonomy with the prefiguration of death. They live as if the limits of their biological life and of their desire no longer applied to them, as if their lifestream had become a geyser endlessly pushing upwards towards the ideal. On the other hand, squanderers flow like country streams: muddy, irregular, voracious and destructive when the flood hits. They take what they want, swallowing treasures and bodies without asking permission. All in all, squanderers prefigure the freedom *of* the flesh, not *from* the flesh.

Having clarified these differences, how are we to understand the perspective of squandering in relation to ourselves? Us – cannon fodder, working flesh, trapped between global capitalism and the nation-state? Certainly very few of us dispose of the material wealth of Sicilian aristocrats, or have the minuscule appetite of the lilies-of-the-field or of the birds in the air. Most of us, in all likelihood, can roughly be classified as part of the impoverished middle class. We are not banned from the job-market, but our jobs are mind-numbing, or physically numbing, exercises of patience and degradation. Thanks to waged-labour or to State Welfare, we might have enough money to feed ourselves and to have a roof over our heads, but never enough to take a break from the perennial quest for survival. If, similarly to Sicilian aristocrats, our wealth is part of the chain that restricts the free enjoyment of our lives, such a chain does not constitute the principal decoy that leads us into the trap of religious obedience. Money – or, to be exact, the lack of thereof – forces us inside our workplaces with the roughness of a prison guard, rather than with the lascivious promises of an ideologue. The violence that it exerts on us produces rage and resentment, not the temptation of obedience. Paradoxically, it is from the feelings produced by our struggle to function within the money system, that we can understand how to re-imagine the practice of squandering as applied to our lives.

Once again, the trap of Work – specifically understood as waged-labour – can function perfectly well as an example.

What can our slavery to money teach us about Work?

First of all, our bondage reminds us of the origin and metamorphoses of Work as a concept. A long process of religious self-delusion has been necessary to pass from the myth of the birth of Work as God's punishment for the original sin, to the infamous slogan crowning the entrance to Nazi concentration camps, 'Work will set you free'. A process which covers the distance between the origin of the French word for Work – *travail*, from the Latin *tripalium*, an instrument of torture to which prisoners were bound and burnt alive – and the contemporary discourse about 'happiness at Work', as developed by many global enterprises. The meagreness of our salaries reminds us of such a distance. It presents the Work universe to us for what it really is: a humiliating, exhausting process which currently seems to be the only way for a person who doesn't come from money to gain the necessary means to live. The violence of working poverty and semi-poverty, while utterly paralysing if pushed to the extreme, helps us to rip the veils that often cover the martyrdom of a working life. It destroys Work's offerings of hope, its manicured landscapes and its heavenly promises. In contemporary, Western societies, Work is an unnecessary yet seemingly unavoidable ordeal, and as such it must be understood and treated by those who wish to disentangle themselves from its *tripalium*.

How are squanderers to enter the world of Work? Differently from punks, they do not enter it with the badge of rebellion stapled to their lips. Punks feel obliged to show their disgust and disagreement, at the cost of losing an opportunity to silently steal from the storeroom and the till. Squanderers dress like employees, smile to customers and bosses like employees. They perform as much as it is requested of them, or, if they are able to, they falsify the books. Always smiling, always cunning. Then, when the lights of the shop are off, when the door to the manager's office is closed, they pillage all they can. They mix whiskey with water, fraud bank transactions, export and sell databases, use till money to bet on horses. They take a nap when no one is watching, they work to the rule, play arcade games on their computers, steal the stock or give it away to their friends. Perfect criminals are not those who rob a million banks in plain daylight, their face uncovered, and get away with it. Perfect criminals are those who are able to hide their theft and are never found out. In fact, one could hardly define them as criminals. Perfect criminals are parasites, hiding within the heart of their hosts, gnawing away softly, night after night, until there is nothing left to take – and then, they move away, to another host. Contemporary squanderers are parasites, who use work as a tool to provide themselves with all they need – or with all they can take. Squanderers might be teacher's pets, if such a behaviour can be advantageous to them, yet they are the first ones to steal from their teacher's purse, as she looks away.

Most importantly, squanderers are disbelievers: their hunger stretches as far as their arms reach, their dreams maintain their shape just as long as a warm breath holds its cloud together in the freezing air. They do not believe in the sanity or sanctity of Work, they do not believe in the redeeming features of a perfect career, they recoil from the smothering hold of the office family. They are liars, atheists, spies, looters. They believe in opportunities, and always test their belief against the harsh judgement of their reason and of their tongue.

Lucid Dreaming

What, in the end, do contemporary squanderers have to squander? Certainly not their meagre worldly possessions. Their fire does not have to reach their rented flats, but the imaginary castles built by the promises of normative abstractions. Their dissipation does not have to aim at their stock of monetary currency, but at that of their hope. Their coffers are filled with hope, ready for them, for us, to squander, as we swap the respectful gaze of the believer with the fast, rapacious glance of the disrespectful opportunist.

Let us apply this method to other fields than the spectral cathedral of Work. Let us point it towards the land of milk and honey, towards the dream of the soldier rotting in the trenches, down to the sad song of the migrant asphyxiating in the hold of a cargo boat: the Motherland. Nothing warms the heart on a cold winter night better than the thought of one's Motherland. It is more than a feeling of geographical belonging. The Motherland is the future collapsed inside out, the prospect of an unknown splendour, which lies as far behind us as the promise of heaven lies ahead of us. In fact, heaven must feel like the Motherland – or possibly, heaven might be the true cast from which our earthly Motherland took its shape. Like all dreams, that of the Motherland whispers in our ears, telling us myths of nostalgia and acceptance, unfolding fables of aggression against her enemies – from now, and forever, also our enemies.

It almost feels unnecessary to challenge the idea of Motherland, of Nation or of ethnic belonging. Such discourses are dreams, nightmares, childish fantasies lurking between the shield of the blanket and the horror of a door left open at night. Contesting the non-reality of dreamlike entities such as the Motherland, would require us to look at them from a place of absolute, incontrovertible reality – such as we never encounter in our mortal lives. We live in dreams, surrounded by dreams. Yet, there is a difference between the hallucination of a wide-eyed dreamer – ready to die for their Motherland-dream – and the practical scepticism of lucid dreaming. Lucid dreamers enter their dreams with a full awareness of the futility of asking themselves any question over reality. All they know is the difference between a good dream and a bad one, between an endless fall and a flight over blooming fields. All they care about is what they can do within their dream, how they can bend it towards their own enjoyment. The Motherland is a dream, everything is a dream. But the Motherland is a dream that pierces the skin of our neck and inserts itself into our bloodstream, delving into the maze of our arteries until it reaches our nerves, slowly substituting its spiderweb into the net of ventricles and neural connections. The Motherland acts as if it was itself a lucid dreamer, whose dreams are us: it acts as if it was itself a subject, and us its objects. It is a ventriloquist's puppet that attempts to take over its creator and to become the master of his master: the King of Kings, like monotheistic Religions define their God. And in fact, the *coup d'état* of the ventriloquist's puppet is the founding act of any religious discourse.

Squanderers thus encounter the Motherland as an insidious opponent, better, as a ruthless competitor on the arena of dreams. They do not question its reality: they slip underneath it and cut the tendons in its paws. Motherland, Ethnicity, Culture: squanderers trample all over these goblins like a horde of horses in a stampede. By crushing them under their feet, they keep them away from their sight: in the land of dreams, what better weapon than oblivion? To their rebellious puppets, they no longer offer their words or their arguments, but the silence of a child grown bored of his old toys.

Is the Motherland the only chessboard on which our legs move in the L-shaped steps of wooden horses? Borders, checkpoints, lines in the sand for which to live and die, surround us from all sides. Some of them we keep particularly close to our hearts: we call them our Identities. Sexual and gender-based identities, consumer tribes, political affiliations, class subjectivation ... Even those who wouldn't lift a finger for their institutional Motherland, would jump into battle to defend their Identity. As they spit over traditional flags – deemed too shop-soiled, too blatantly religious – they congregate under the waving rags of other, more contemporary flags. Eventually, they spend so long waving their flags in the wind that they end up becoming their poles. They don't fight against their oppressors as hungry, enraged mortals, but as the part of the Proletariat; they don't struggle against their abusers as vulnerable flesh, but as Women; they don't reclaim their space of freedom and choice as desiring bodies, but as Homosexuals; and so on. They never exist for themselves, but only as representation of something else, of something 'bigger' than themselves: they are the million replicas of the cross, sold for a penny each on the stairway to church.

Squandering, on the contrary, is the act of forgetting how to build flags, while burning those in existence. The only flag squanderers wave is the shadow they cast as they walk along their path. Their only motherland is their own body, and their territory is the world onto which they can have potency. Their world, we said, not the Globe. Missionaries of the *propaganda fidei*, financial transactions and the ambitions of imperialism created the Globe: an abstract grid of geometries, as flat and smooth as the pages of an atlas, the plane of existence of Humanity and ideas. No country for real people. Perhaps that is precisely why the Globe is so easy to cut up with straight lines and divided into Nation-states. Those who live on the Globe let their bodies melt into the immense abstraction of the atlas, as if their imaginary knowledge of the objective existence of places they will never see was enough for them to claim them as part of their personal habitat. Those who think of themselves as Globe-dwellers bind themselves forever to the fate of deficient drawing tools on God's drawing desk. There is no room for humans on the Globe, only for Humanity. Any territory that exceeds our possibilities of potency over it is a dream from which we are excluded, or in which we are only allowed as objects.

Squanderers, like animals, claim for themselves only what can possibly be theirs. They live in their own world. And a 'world' has nothing to do with immortal geometries. The Italian, French, Spanish and Portuguese terms for 'world' all derive from the Latin *locus mundus*, meaning the place which is 'adorned', 'clean' and 'visible'. The world is the place which goes under the influence of those who adorn it and make it their own – that is, clean to their taste, even though this process often happens by soiling it, – those who can see it with their own eyes. Borrowing from the Greek, we might say that our world is our home, as in *oikonomia*, the art of imposing an order (*nomos*) to our home (*oikos*). How distant is this conception of economics from the contemporary practices of capitalism? How remote is it from industrial planning? Global, industrial economics are the space of action of governments and multinational lobbies: game rooms to which you, and I, and most of those we know, will never be allowed. The engine of global dreams is powerful and terrifying, yet its control is far away from us. Possibly, only its partial destruction is within our reach.

When talking about this type of *oiko-nomia*, we might want to be careful not to be misled by the word 'home', as it should not lead us to believe that the world of the squanderers necessarily coincides with small, local communities. Many of them, like many of us, experience their world as an intricate game of near remoteness and distant closeness. The world, for each one of us, is the dreamscape – which often includes the digital infoscape – in which we can act, and which we can change. Worlds, like islands, often change their shape: as the tide rises and sinks, also the boundaries of our world transform. As the strength of our arms increases, the beach of our island dries the sea that surrounds it; as weakness overcomes us, the shore recedes, and seagulls have to build their nests higher up on the rocks.

3

The Wheels of History

I remember their batons. Why weren't they shooting their guns at us? I remember the silence of the windows lined up along the path of the march. Where was the civil society we were meant to be talking to? We were showing our banners to each other, chanting our slogans to keep the cold of winter at bay. We were acting out a play compressed in two minutes of a TV news report, stuck in a role cut out for other epochs, for bodies that weren't ours.

While some of us decided to change the world with yoga sessions, some others planned to do it with organised marches of millions and called the masses to action. And millions showed up. And they were as effective as the drum circles of the yoga veterans.

We thought that we were doing politics, while we were playing the historic re-enactment of a vision of the 20th Century. The police beat us with their rubber sticks, like puppets beat each other in a village play. There was nothing serious about us, or about them.

Sometimes, somebody died. But that didn't matter. It never really mattered. They died by mistake, fighting a mock battle with wooden swords. We declared a war we weren't willing or able to fight, and our opponents laughed at our cloth banners and at our facepaint, treating us as the children we were. Rubber batons, half-hearted horse charges, police notices. We thought it was a war, and it was a pantomime. Sometimes, some of us smashed a window. But even that didn't matter. It never really mattered. They threw their incendiary, representational acts against the representations of their opponents, as if in a fistfight between portraits.

The wheels of history are tracing new paths over our lives, crushing the dirt roads that we used to trust and call our own. Yet, here we stand, heroically croaking toads, stubbornly deluded about the power of our protest.

Representative democracy is not suspended, it is a historical relic. It is over. That dream is over. Today, the space of politics in the West is that of a play in which even real blood looks fake, in which the death of the actors only gains applauses and tears, but never even manages to derail the sliding of the stage curtain.

Maybe, in the future – a future that is likely to escape us – the wheels of history will take a different path. Maybe they will even break down. Maybe, then, people like us will be in the position of gaining access to the game rooms of politics, without having necessarily to pass through the nightly blasts of dynamite. And maybe, once again, it will be the time for the heroism of open battlefields. But for now, we should take the measures of the place we are in, and of the time in which we live. This is not the time for assaults, but for withdrawal. This is not time for war, but for revenge – silent, cruel, ghostly.

On the stage in which we are either tools or managers of representations, we might want to become the silent rats, gnawing the curtains when the lights go off at night. In the zoo in which we are either prisoners or guardians, we might want to become stray dogs, stealing food from cages, biting security when they fall asleep. Of all the glowing costumes we are offered – lined with hopes and chains – today we might want to choose the invisible clothes of the parasite.

A Parasite's Civilisation

A Tailor's Work

We already mentioned Civilisation in the course of our discussion over the birth of immortality and of normative abstractions. Admittedly, our brief characterisation of the concept wasn't imbued with particularly positive acceptations. The position that we assigned to Civilisation was that of the earthly implementer and manager of the Kingdom of Normative Abstractions. Our description of their relationship resembled that which exists between a local Mafia tenant and his Mafia 'Don', whose heavenly rule the tenant is called to bring into practice within the territory that is assigned to him. Immortal, normative abstractions set the unreachable goals and unmeetable standards, which Civilisation ensures are duly and painfully chased by those living under its heel.

However, we must now be more specific. What defines a Civilisation, as opposed to a general congregation of people, organisms or ideas? Why did we connect it to the origin and, indeed, to the essence of religious thought and practice?

If we look at Civilisation from a nearer distance, we might be surprised by our inability to spot it anywhere as a specific object. Civilisation does not exist like 'things' do: it is not a specific idea, a specific object, or a specific group of people or of objects. The reason for our inability to find the object named Civilisation, is that Civilisation operates and exists only as a connection between people, ideas, objects and so on. We could say that Civilisation does not exist as an indivisible 'atom' (from the Greek *a-tome*, 'that which cannot be cut'), but rather as a specific type of conjuncture between 'atoms'. If we were to compare it to a biological formation, we could say that Civilisation is one of the many possible arrangements of a multitude of cells, or, even better, a specific cellular conjuncture of sub-cellular units.

How can we define this specific conjuncture, which constitutes the essence of Civilisation? We can approach this question by observing certain types of bonds existing between words, which are at work in literature. In particular, we can focus on those conglomerates of literary conjunctures that go under the names of 'novel' and 'dictionary.' Within a novel, words are carefully chosen and connected one to the other, according to a transparent narrative intent. The words that are excluded – that is, not bound to the others – are those that do not fit within the narrative that the author desires to unfold. By stitching and cutting words, authors build specific structures of sense – Civilisations, we might say – which define and are defined by their territory, their internal dynamics, their population, and so on. Despite the apparent difference between genres, the same process is at work within a dictionary. Like a novel, a dictionary is a web of connections and exclusions, which describes the immense meta-narrative of a whole language. In a sense, we might even say that a dictionary precedes and allows the narrative of a novel, since it builds the general narrative of the language on which the novel relies.

What is a narrative?

The essence of a narrative is the double act of combining a number of elements and entities – supposedly neutral and senseless in themselves – and, at the same time, of containing them within an object (most often, a virtual, immaterial object) which defines their boundaries, their scope and, ultimately, their meaning. The creation of a narrative is the work of a tailor who cuts and binds, connects and excludes, with the aim of bringing into the world an object that did not and could not exist without the tailor's wilful intervention. In this sense, we can interpret Civilisation as the process of tailoring an as-yet-inexistent shape out of the supposedly shapeless galaxy of humans, landscapes, interactions, interpretations, and so on.

Since the beginning of History – that is, since the birth of abstract immortality – Civilisation's various social and cultural narratives have characterised the presence of humans on Earth. Nations and empires have endlessly divided the globe, moulding the senseless magma of life and land into an extraordinary catalogue of shapes, according to one or another grand structure of sense, may it be the godly design of theocracies or the historical necessities of secular powers. The word Civilisation thus describes the work of an invisible artisan, tirelessly re-orienting human and natural life towards a superior, abstract horizon, and, in doing so, ultimately submitting it to the immortal dominion of normative abstractions.

Civilisations of the Self

We talked about Civilisation as the work of a tailor, but who is this 'invisible tailor' we referred to?

As in the example of local Mafia tenants – which we compared with really existing Civilisations – who is this ghostly equivalent of a Mafia 'Don', whose power they represent on Earth?

During our earlier discussion about Religion and radical atheism, we identified this entity as that of a normative abstraction. Now, after our brief exploration of the connections between Civilisation and narrative, we can expand our description of what a normative abstraction is and how it acts over human lives. *Normative abstraction* is the name that we can use to define an idea or a set of ideas which individuals or collectives place above themselves as the ultimate frame and scope of reference for their earthly existences. When applied to human collectivities, the actual translation of the structure of sense of a normative abstraction (we could say, its potential narrative) into the materiality of human and natural life (that is, its actual narrative) can be described as the process of a Civilisation. In this sense, we can identify a number of normative abstractions that, throughout history, have given rise to as many Civilisations: God and theocracies, Progress and communisms, Humanity and liberalisms, and so on. Most often, Civilisations have acted as the servants of two or more masters, bringing into practice a combination of the immortal designs of several normative abstractions.

If we zoom past the grand scale of human Civilisations and closer to the microcosms of specific human collectivities, we find the same dynamic at play in the field commonly defined as populism. Although often mistaken for a merely derogative political adjective, populism is the political phenomenon which produces a convergence of several different demands – often seemingly irreconcilable with each other – into one, abstract umbrella-concept, which acts as an empty container (or, more precisely, an empty signifier) capable of holding them all together within one form. This empty signifier – often symbolised by a flag or a slogan – exists as a normative abstraction, and acts as the political equivalent of a Civilisation over the demands that it contains, binding them together and ultimately re-defining them in terms that exceed the original. Like the combination of normative abstractions and Civilisation, the umbrella of a populist empty signifier exists and acts as an invisible tailor, sewing together, cutting away, creating shapes and tight clothes within which to contain human lives.

Why did we expand our exploration of normative abstractions and Civilisations to the seemingly remote shores of political populism?

The reason for this detour lies in the perhaps surprising parallel between such dynamics and the unfolding of our mortal, fragile, individual lives. The narrative game enacted by normative abstractions, populist empty signifiers and Civilisations does not only take place outside of, but also inside us. Like the wide face of the Earth itself, our own existential and psychological territories are traversed by and crammed with countless populations, which are not composed of humans but of our drives, desires, needs, dreams, etc. And as it occurs with human populations, Civilisations rise and fall also inside us, empty signifiers appear and disappear, and normative abstractions struggle to control our inner world.

Similarly to the very planet on which we exist, each one of us lives as a biosphere: cycles of renewal act as both enhancers and limits to our possibilities of action, our aims have to be compared with available resources, and the spectrum of the possible varies according to the level of organisation of the efforts that we are able to put into place. It is under this lens that we should observe the presence of Civilisations and normative abstractions within our existential functioning.

Despite our critical position towards the social implementation of the regimes of Civilisations throughout history and our acknowledgment of its costs, it is undeniable that the coordinated effort of multitudes of humans – bound together under the umbrella of one or the other normative abstraction – has led the human consortium to improve dramatically its living conditions. The same acknowledgement should be applied to the sphere of our inner, psychological lives. If left to themselves, what would the hordes of desires, drives and dreams existing within us, ultimately do? Would they recreate the idyllic utopia of imagined hunter-gatherer communities, or would they rather enact a terrifying mix of environmental devastation and paralysis of action? It is exactly in order for the potential of our inner populations to fully flourish – within and compatibly to our inner environment and resources – that a level of coordination among them becomes extremely useful. How can such hordes create a functional union between themselves, aimed at the actual implementation of their demands in the sphere of so-called 'real' life? As we have already pointed out, populism is exactly the name that is employed in political sciences to describe an empty signifier – that is, a vessel that in itself is nothing but empty – which is capable of enhancing such a union between absolutely different and seemingly irreconcilable entities and demands. In order for them to exist as more than simple inner fantasies, our desires, needs and dreams necessitate some sort of structured form of collectivity, something like an empty signifier able to represent them. In other words, they require a normative abstraction, something that is above them and transcends them, while re-shaping and re-addressing their action towards a set of practical goals and aims.

What is this normative abstraction that they erect above themselves, like the frogs of the fable, asking for a king to rule over them? For once, the answer is truly easy: it is us. 'I', that is, my 'self', is such a normative abstraction and empty signifier. I am the hologram of the totem around which my desires, drives and dreams congregate, I am the literary artifice which allows them to put aside their differences and achieve some sort of functioning union. I, as such, do not exist: I am the populist fiction of my inner world, I function as its Civilisation. We are Civilisations of our own selves, and, as such, we rise and collapse, cyclically scarring our existential territories with the marks of recurrent apocalypses. In order to exist and function as 'selves', we need to exert a religious, manipulating and often coercive control over the hordes that populate *us*. As the invisible tailors of our own inner narrative and Civilisation, our intent is that of acquiring a certain degree of control over them and, ultimately, to reduce them as much as possible into submission to us. When they rebel, we can either fight them or negotiate; when they defeat us, we undergo a transformation; and when they simply desert and break away from us, we are declared insane.

Us Parasites

It is because of our familiarity with the *modus operandi* of Civilisations and of normative abstractions – in fact, it is exactly because we function and exist as normative abstractions and Civilisations ourselves – that we grow so suspicious of the normative abstractions of social life, of their religious methods and of their 'civilising' attempts. When faced by Culture, Society, Religion, the State and so on, we are faced by our equals. We know how they want to include us within their scheme, because that is exactly what we do to our internal populations. We recognise the functional utility of a civilised structure, yet, as individual, rebellious, autonomous entities, we desire not to submit to the plan of their 'greater necessity'.

Yet what options do we have, if we don't want to submit? Sometimes, through what goes under the name of a 'revolutionary transformation', it might seem possible to fight against the specific, immaterial masters which, at a certain time, rule over us. Yet, is it ever really possible to defeat our immaterial masters *tout-court*? As well as killing the king, can we also destroy once and for all the throne on which he sits? Or is it rather the case that the immortality of normative abstractions actually consists in the fact that they always come back, although in different form? Is the social and political struggle against normative abstractions and Civilisation – that is, the project of social autonomy – a project that is at all possible? And if it isn't, what other option do we have?

In order to understand which options are open to us, we must begin by understanding what goals we have, in our dealing with the social Civilisation in which we exist, and with the normative abstractions that regulate social life. As noted earlier, as well as tragic disadvantages, social Civilisations have undoubtedly brought terrific advantages to the life of those who live beneath their heel: from medical and scientific progress, to the provision of public services, to global communications and so on. Are we really sure that, for a desire of a radically atheist freedom, we are available to renounce all advantages brought to us by Civilisation? Also, and paradoxically, wouldn't that become a religious position in itself?

Radical atheism and the practice of squandering do not aim at a total purity of their 'adepts', nor do they incite a celestial pauperism. If Civilisation has something to offer to squanderers, they will not refuse to take it for themselves – provided, of course, that they can manage to get away without having to pay for it, or at least not dearly.

It is easy to bring an example of such a seemingly incoherent and, indeed, hypocritical position, if we consider the relationship between squanderers and public healthcare. Public healthcare, as it exists nowadays, is the direct emanation of a Nation State and originates from a chain of Civilisations that can be roughly traced back to the set of normative abstractions belonging to the philosophy of the Enlightenment. Almost everything about it, in theory, should persuade squanderers to keep away from it. Yet, if the objective of a squanderer's life is to enjoy their time on this planet to the fullest, and to make their potential flourish completely, wouldn't such an objective be hindered by a complete lack of access to public healthcare? Especially for those squanderers who cannot access a wealth of material resources, State-provided services are essential, despite their murky ideological implications. Yet, how can we define the attitude of a squanderer towards such useful though dangerous, institutions? Clearly, squanderers are not legitimate users of these facilities. Squanderers cannot define themselves as loyal citizens, entitled to services such as State-provided healthcare on the basis of their belief in the promise of the State and of his set of dominant abstractions. Nor they are customers, since their occasional – but ever increasing – acceptance to pay for cures does not derive from a wilful and autonomous 'consumer choice' but by urgent biological necessities. We must find or invent another category that can aptly describe a squanderer's behaviour in reference to those social institutions that are useful to them. We already briefly defined this category – or, better, this position – as that of the parasite: now, in order to expand our understanding of it and to describe the passages that lead to it, we may continue by telling a fable.

Metamorphoses of Rebellion – A Fable

Once upon a time, there was a mule that prided himself on how much weight he could carry. He especially enjoyed carrying the enormous silver statues and candelabras used in the local church during religious festivities. His back was covered with sores, festering under the leather strips that connected the baskets on his sides, but he took little notice of them. Only one thing bothered him. Even in the agony of climbing up Mount Calvary fully loaded, on Easter Friday, the weight on his back didn't seem heavy enough. The pleasure he derived from the pain was too brief, its promises too narrow to include his dream of ever reaching anywhere higher than the pinnacle of pain and pleasure at the top of the Mount. He began spending his nights wide-eyed, incessantly praying for a sign, a hint, a direction to point his desires towards. As it is known, Gods in fables are merciful and cruel, and his prayers did not fall to a deaf ear. One morning, just as Easter was ending and his services were destined to fall into short demands for some time, at the exit of his stable he encountered a sheep. The sheep greeted him joyously. "How can you smile, sheep," asked the mule, "after you saw your master killing one of your lambs and serving his roasted carcass to his guests?" The sheep continued savouring her smile for a while then replied with warm and smooth voice "Dear mule, how could I not smile? My master had to do what he did, my son had to be killed and eaten. And I, as far as my insignificant life is concerned, have to keep on smiling, and to keep on breeding roast dinners for my master to eat." Maybe because of his melancholy at the end of his glorious time as a carrier of the cross, the mule felt a pang of compassion for the sheep. "You truly sound resigned to your fate, dear sheep, I am so sorry for you," he said sympathetically. The sheep calmly shook her woolly head and stretched her smile even wider. "I am not resigned, mule. I am joyous, I am complete. I do what I must, and by doing so, what must happen finally includes me too. I was given a life worth nothing and look at me now, I can aspire to be part of something so much bigger than myself, something that includes everything you see around you. Everything must be, and I want it to be so. I must, and I want."

That night the mule didn't pray, but once again he could not sleep. He kept stamping his hooves against the dust and hay covering the floor, repeating to himself the words of the sheep. Dawn found him still awake, his eyes striped with thick red veins. "I must, I want, I want to must," he said to the first light of day. When his master opened the stable in the morning, the mule didn't feel any sadness for the lack of load and his wounded pride. Whatever was going to happen to him, it must have happened, and he wanted it to happen. He greeted his master with a smile and, pacing slowly, like a sheep would stroll on a luscious carpet of grass, he started to walk towards the end of the village. Humans had warned him of the dangers that hid in the forest at the end of the road, but he forgot all their recommendations. He kept walking on, still repeating his new mantra.

Certainly, a smiling mule is a rare sight in this world, and even more so one lost in deep meditation. But surprise lasted on the wolf's jaws only long enough for his drooling to wash it away. With the rapacious violence that made him infamous, the wolf jumped out of the shrubbery, landing teeth first on the mule's neck. As the blood spread thick and rusty, the bubble of silence that sometimes surrounds a sudden death fell onto our two characters, enveloping them. Inside it, the mule's mantra alone resounded, feebly leaking out his mouth. "I must, I want, I want to must." The wolf tore his victim's warm flesh and licked his lips. "What nonsense!" he commented, as the mule spent his last breath to finally repeat his formula.

That was a good day for the wolf, and the sun was shining and the stream nearby was roaring with fresh and sweet water. But the life of a wolf is rarely dotted by such beautiful days. The rain soon came, and then the snow. After they heard of the fate of the mule, villagers started to carry weapons on their way into the forest, and expeditions were organised to find the murderer of the mule and to bring him to justice. The wolf kept low for some time, hiding in the depth of the forest. He even started to eat berries and leaves, waiting for the villagers' hysteria to fade away. Unfortunately for him, however, those weren't yet the fast-paced times of media hysterias. Villagers kept looking for days, weeks, months. Winter fell heavily on the forest and even berries and leaves became scarce. The wolf thought of entering the village in disguise to steal some food, but his features were too well known by everyone for him to ever feel safe under any camouflage. His fame preceded him, and now condemned him to starvation. Time passed, though it felt like it never did. The wolf felt the shivers of winter running under his fur, and visions of blood spraying in front of his eyes. He ran around in circles, tracing ring-paths in the snow, to keep the cold at bay. "Am I to die like an idiot, like one of those villagers when they get lost in the forest?" He stopped, and his breath shined under the light of the moon. He frowned and sunk his claws into the snow. "I am a wolf, I am a fighter! I can take them, I can eat their fear off their faces! They'll see!" The wolf raised his eyes at the moon and bit his tongue until it bled, to give himself the taste of victory.

From then on, all that happened cannot be described through the eyes of the wolf. He could no longer see. Even before he entered the village, even before the first peasant took the first shot with his rifle, even before the blade of another villager's knife cut the fur off his skin, the wolf could no longer see what was around him. Starvation and anger, like sandstorms, turn all colours to one. It is through other eyes, that is, through the eyes of a survivor, that we can see what happened next. The dog had been in the village for all his life. He didn't belong to anybody, yet always managed to take food from every kitchen. He had been kicked at times, and at times he had had to sleep in the cold. But over the years he had learnt his way through the broken fences and into the barns left open at night. When the wolf entered the village drooling ravenously, the dog looked at him from a distance, with the uncertainty of spotting a fast-shooting star. The wolf had always been something of a hero to him. Living free in the woods, eating any sheep that ventured too deep into the shrubbery, even occasionally biting the odd young shepherd, asleep under a tree. That was no life for the dog, but the wolf – ah! – the wolf was living all the dog's dreams on his behalf. When the first peasant shot, the dog jolted, as if the bullet that cracked the wolf's skull had hit him instead. As the snow around the wolf melted under the warm flow of his blood, the dog stared intently at the villagers gathered around the moribund body. He took note of every face. A father cut the wolf's tail with his knife and gave it to his child to play with. The dog took note of both their faces.

That night, the village had a great feast, in celebration of the just killing of a public enemy. Despite the bitter cold, villagers took their tables out of their homes and brought them to the square, surrounding the banquet with a circle of lit torches. There was roasted meat, potatoes, parsnip, bread, cheese, ale and wine. The dog waited for the commensals to hit an adequate level of drunkenness, before nipping in and out of the circle of torches, stealing all he could, sometimes taking the offers of the diners, sometimes even playing tricks at their request, to please them. He ate among them, wagged his tail when appropriate, and drank soup from their plates. More wine was brought out, more ale and bottles of spirits. Some of the men returned home with their wives, others fell asleep on their chairs. The child who had been given the wolf's tail was still playing with it, sitting on his father's lap. The man was drunk, fast asleep. The torches began to run out of fuel. The dog licked the child's hand, wagged his tail, run out of the circle of light and barked. The child was delighted; not only he was being allowed to stay up longer than usual, but he could even play with the dog! He jumped off his father's lap and followed the dog out of the circle. The dog walked back to the child, licked his hand once more and once more run a bit further, towards the end of the village. The child ran after him. A bit further. Almost at the point in which the wolf had been killed. There, the darkness was so thick that the child could no longer see where he was moving his steps. The dog could feel the child's joy quickly fading. He could hear his sobbing rising in his chest. A few more seconds, and his crying would call the attention of one of the villagers. The child kept the wolf's tail tightly in his hand, even when the dog clenched his jaws around his throat. When he cried, it was only the dog's mouth that heard him. Sinking his teeth in the child's flesh, the dog thought about the wolf, then about the trimmings taken from the child's hands, just a few minutes ago. The child's body shook once, violently, then no more. The dog walked to the end of the road, towards the forest. When he reached the shrubbery, where the snow ended and his traces could no longer be found, he howled at the moon

– almost as a joke, almost as a mournful cry.

The air was fresh and crispy, the moon was bright. He took a long detour through the forest, then strolled back towards the village. He passed through the usual maze of holes in the fences, back to the barn where the hay was the softest. He curled up and licked his paws. When he closed his eyes, a quick though crossed his mind. That was the barn of the child's family. Sleep came on tiptoes, like a lover hiding in the night. The dog smiled, and let it wrap itself around him.

4

The Word

I have often encountered a problem, when talking or writing about radical atheism. While busy producing my own proclamations against the strangulating regimes of dominant abstractions, or against the sacrifice of one's life that they enforce, I found that the alternative that I was able to offer did not match their narrative and evocative qualities.

Although annihilating in practice, dominant abstractions are able to offer their disciples a frame of sense from within which their lives can unfold as complete narratives. How could I think of encouraging people to abandon the poisonous environment of religious submission, if all I had to offer as an alternative was the desert of a vague freedom, of a 'fullness of life', which I couldn't even explain?

At the same time I was aware of the fact that, if I had fallen into the temptation of creating yet another abstraction, I would have simply replicated the very enemy against which I was willing to fight. I needed to find an alternative that was flexible, malleable and docile enough, so not to replicate the constricting grids of the currently existing abstract systems.

The alternative I was looking for had to have a name, for the simple reason that people pass from home to home, and from name to name. Its name had to be not as strong as another -ism, but not as weak as an adjective. A noun, then. But not any noun. 'Freedom' for example, is a noun that announces itself as a radical emptiness. Perfect in theory, useless in practice. When entering a new home, a person wants to find it empty, but not without a floor or a roof. I needed another noun, capable of being at the same time empty and present enough.

As one does when faced by a difficult problem, I looked into my daily life in search of an answer. Friendship, then, felt like a good ground to start my investigation. There was always something that allowed me to distinguish between the long list of unmemorable relationships and the few who were to remain. In all my strongest friendships, in all the best relationships I have ever had, an element seemed to constantly recur. It was the feeling of a movement together with the other person, a tension towards something or somewhere, a common action, a sense of solidarity within the frame of a shared intent. The people I have ever felt closest to have been something more than friends: they have been comrades.

Of course, I accept the political connotation of the word. But with a difference. Like political comrades, we were bound by a common desire and a common tension. Differently from them, however, our desires and tensions could not be limited by the dogma of some abstract ideals, let alone pre-existing ideologies. Between us, there was *something* that originated from us alone.

That still motion between us was exactly *it*, the noun I was trying to look for.

What was it, then?

Apart from in my friendships, I have encountered *it* in other places, in which I never set foot but with my mind. In books, in films, in stories I met *it* countless times. And *it* had a name, then. A name so common, so simple, and that we all have long known. In those books that I used to read as a child, *it* was clearly stated, as a whole literary genre.

Finally, I found *it*.

It was *adventure*.

Adventure!

Adventure

The Skeleton

We have found the word, and now we hold it in our hands. We don't have long to decide how to structure our relationship with it. Words are dangerous things. One minute they are in your hand, the other they are flying above your head, pointing at a direction, biting your ears the moment you attempt to disobey their orders. Or they wrap themselves around you, and the softness of their sound hardly hides the tightness of their corset.

When they first appear in our own private universe, words have the simple shape of containers. Containing meaning is what they are supposed to do, and their shape presents itself accordingly.

The first few moments after we get hold of a new and fascinating word, it is still too dark to understand the nature and thickness of its substance. We feel its sides on a skin level, trying to perceive their texture, the smoothness or roughness of their finish, whether their edges are polished, or if their bottom is wet. Yet, it is while still in the dark that we must bet on the most important aspect of a word's nature: whether its sides are opaque or transparent.

Most words, upon touching human hands, turn into impenetrably opaque containers. Their sides can be of any colour of the spectrum, but they surely have one that is of their own. Colour transmits, faster than diseases. Although it should be meaning that infuses words, it often happens that the meaning we pour into a word ends up taking the word's colour: after all, the moment water is poured, it assumes the colour of the cup.

Thus in reference to our new word, do we want to pour ourselves into the cup of the word 'adventure', only to assume its colour? Wouldn't that be the ultimate – indeed, the essential – religious and submissive gesture towards a newly born normative abstraction?

We want the sides of our new word to be transparent, like glass. We want ourselves to be darker than water, and our meaning to be liquid dye. Adventure will be for us a docile, useful, available tool. A transparent glass then, into which to pour the flow of our acts and meanings, so to make them understandable to ourselves and communicable to others.

Yet a glass still has sides, though transparent. It has its own limits, which include and exclude: any action, thought or feeling that exceeds its boundaries is irrevocably banned from its territory. Or, at least, this is how normal words function. But adventure is in our hands like a piece of paper. We can cut it, fold it, make an origami out of it. We can even invert the rules that normally apply to other words, and turn its boundaries inside out, or, more precisely, outside in.

We said that words are containers, designed to carry meaning around. But what shape should a container have, if its function is no longer that of a semiotic vessel, but of an existential one? Would a cup or a glass really be a suitable container for the flow of unpredictable, autonomous, unique lives? Luckily, we don't have to answer this question all on our own. Natural evolution has already been confronted by this same dilemma, and has provided us with examples of another, possible answers. As opposed to the containing shell of an exoskeleton, which structures and limits the flesh from the outside, more recent forms of life have developed the internal structure of an endoskeleton, or, as it is commonly know, a skeleton.

Adventure can thus become a skeleton, that is, a scaffolding of bones that would enhance the movements of our muscles, the stretching and contracting of our limbs all around it. As with any word, it still has limits but, differently from what happens with container-like words, these no longer belong to the geographical dimension of perimeters. The limits of such a word are the dynamics of the internal equilibrium of a three-dimensional object: they are a function of its barycentre. Adventure expands and shrinks, rises and lowers, in accord with the movements of our life. The relationship between the word and the flesh no longer is the normative constriction of religion and ideology, but becomes the cooperative relationship between bones and muscles, joints and nerves.

Adventure is the skeleton, around which we wrap ourselves as soft, sensitive, desiring flesh.

Our expedition thus has to become the journey of an anatomist's eye. We know the flesh, with the intuitive certainty of pain and pleasure, but what are the shapes of the bones? What are they for? How do they enhance and limit our movements?

The orthopaedics of adventure, if we may call it so, is still a very young discipline. Our catalogue of bones might be lacking, incomplete, at times possibly plain wrong. By no means it wishes to present itself as a complete and dogmatic list. Like every encyclopaedia, its pages are made of tearable paper and its edges are blank and ready to be covered in notes and corrections.

Time

At the heart of each bone, as if it was their marrow, we find the temporal essence of any life that wishes to revolve around adventure. Like marrow, the time of adventure is tender, moist and painful. Adventurers only exist within the time of their own mortality. No heaven or hell, no memory or glory lie beyond the moment in which their bodies start rotting. The time of adventure only exists as a 'time of now', that is as the only possible, available moment in which the invisible populations of our inner civilisation can put their plans to practice. Whatever we desire, we can only achieve within the narrow time of our biology.

If the time of Work expands as seemingly limitless as a desert, that of adventure exists as a limited, often frustratingly small, patch of an oasis. Before and beyond us is only the bleak wake of galaxies and dark matter. Similarly to the planet we live on, our lives have to considered as the fragile, implausible occurrences of a mistake within an indifferent universe.

Yet, if such bleakness and fragility might be too much for us to bear, the time of adventure also provides a warmer, deeper space in which our lives can unfold. As with every oasis, the centre of a life of adventure is the depth of the well that connects the surface to the spring. The time of adventure might only stretch a few decades in breadth, but it sinks almost infinitely in depth.

While the time of Religion and Work proceeds along a horizontal, historical series of achievements – in accordance with the set of expectations of one normative abstraction or the other – the time of adventure flows along the sinuous track of the event.

What is an event? As our life path meets the trajectories of the populations of our inner civilisation, an event occurs. As the energy of our actions meets the direction of our desires, the 'evental' explosion that occurs translates into the speed of adventure-time. It is this propellant energy that pushes the time of adventure deeper and deeper under the crust of traditional, linear, clock-time. While the time of History spreads on the surface, turning everything it finds on its path into a desert – often desiccating millions of oases at once under the sandstorm of war and repression – the time of adventure seeks new possibilities of expansion along the mole-roads opened by the event.

Risk

After exploring the inner workings of the bones of adventure, let us focus on their external, bleached-white contours. How impenetrable or porous is their surface?

The process of approaching one's surface – that is, one's limits – can be described as a movement towards what exceeds oneself. As one approaches what exists outside of oneself, one nears the territory of danger. Far from being simply descriptive of what may cause ruin, danger encompasses all that escapes our control. Danger might lead to disaster, as well as to new pleasures. It is a matter of risk, rather than of plain doom.

Taking risks thus means running the distance to the limits of one's skin, until the point of contact with the outside. By taking risks, we not only allow ourselves to explore the outside, but we also allow the outside to enter us. As it happens with debt and credit, one's exit from one's limits (the obtainment of credit) coincides with the invasion of what is external to oneself (the chains of debt). We can easily see the equivalence of this reciprocal penetration of inside and outside, if we consider one's relationship with others. Upon initiating interaction with an other, this process of reciprocal trespassing begins. Several strategies have been put into place over the millennia, so to make such a process as little traumatic as possible – let us think for example about the strategies of politeness and formality – yet the substance of this double penetration still remains at the heart of every social interaction. The moment this temporary intercourse becomes permanent, as it happens with the creation of a 'social contract', interaction turns into a bond. As it happens after sex among several animal species, the pleasure of the intercourse often suddenly turns into the embarrassing position of being forcefully stuck to each other.

It is for this reason that adventurers, perhaps surprisingly, maintain a very prudent attitude towards risk. When they are asked to join a group or a community, or to enter into a relationship of deep interaction with random partners – as it often happens, for example, in workplaces or local communities – they always consider the possible consequences of a bonding penetration. In particular, it is on this grounds that adventurers restrain from taking part in any collective gatherings around any totem dedicated to dominant abstractions such as ethnic, national, gender or class Identities: the chain of hands which encircles the totem, it is now clear, is the prototype for another, harder, metallic kind of chain.

The Union of Egoists

Having observed the bones, let us focus on the cartilage that holds them together.

Adventurers' prudence towards community-making does not mean that adventure has to be a solitary experience. Although lone riding allows a number of pleasures, cooperation is certainly an enormous enhancer of any possibilities of enjoyment of life. What distinguishes adventure from all forms of Religion – from the traditional ones to those of neoliberalism or of State communism – is the type of structure that characterises cooperation within it.

Cooperation, within adventure, is always a slow, autonomous and negotiating process. There is no 'moral imperative' which compels adventurers to become companions: any union which takes place within adventure always derives from, and is aimed exclusively at, the satisfaction of the needs, desires and aims of its members. Within adventure, unions cannot pre-exist nor transcend the specific members which constitute them: as members come and go – and the possibility of leaving such alliances at any time is of the utmost importance – unions change shape, readjusting to the new balance of interests which compose them.

We could call them 'unions of egoists', in the sense that the interests of each Civilisation, belonging to each members of such unions, act as the only rationale for the costs and the risk-taking involved in the instatement of a bond between the members.

Clearly, not all members of a union have in practice the same influence within it. Different people have different charisma, or different talents. Yet, it is crucial to stress how unions of egoists are federations whose members are at the same time deeply unique in themselves and equal to each other. The bonds of comradeship do not leave any space for institutional roles of dominion. The occasional leadership assumed by one member or the other is not defined in permanent terms, but simply resembles the alternative primacy of one leg over the other when walking.

As it always happens with the creation of a bond, unions of egoists necessarily result in something that exceeds a friendship based on shared interests or the simple joint-venture of cooperating forces. This 'surplus', which originates from the creation of a bond of comradeship between adventurers, is the consequence of the way the bones of adventure grow over time together with the flesh of life. We shall discuss this aspect next.

Comradeship

As it happens with a body, as time passes and the flesh expands, bones also have to grow in strength and size. How does adventure undergo such a process of growth?

As we already observed a few pages ago, adventurers, like all humans, live within a dream, in which they try to be the lucid dreamers. The reality that surrounds them is a landscape, the ontological proof of which is unobtainable. Yet, this said reality is the only one in which they – we – are bound to exist, and which constantly affects us with its friction against our inner, existential territory. We described the process of lucid dreaming as the active, wilful, yet sceptical life of an individual within such an uncertain reality. Now we must add another element to our description.

So far, we have discussed the possibility of action of one individual within reality. But what happens if this individual joins forces with others? Cooperative action within the dreamscape of reality opens a range of possibilities that would be unobtainable by solitary action. In this sense – and since the modification of one's environment becomes part of the process of the influence that the said environment has on the person – the expansion of one's potency within reality, via the creation of a union of egoists, constitutes the essential growth of the bones of adventure. Comradeship among egoists allows them to further modify the reality in which they exist, thus shaping the landscape of their adventure and taming at least in part the influence that the environment in which they exist has on them.

Such a process, like the presence of cartilage in between bones, is crucial for setting the range of movements that a body can possibly enact. Since we described the dreamscape of reality as a territory in which people exist, we could describe the movements performed within it as explorations. We are talking about a kind of exploration which predates the modern voyages of rational, cartographic discovery, and which refers instead to the medieval habit of mythopoeic travelling.

As with travellers of the dark ages, or Aborigines along the Song Lines, adventurers explore their landscape with a motion that produces the land on which their travelling unfolds. Possibly out of all needs, that of creating such an immense landscape is the main force bringing adventurers together and encouraging them to associate in unions of egoists. Creating an entire reality, producing a whole new ecosystem of enactable dreams, is too big a task for one person alone.

War and Empathy

What sound do such bones produce?

Within adventure, not only the intermittent beeping of Work is absent, but so is also the reassuring, background humming typical of dominant abstractions. Adventurers are aware of the fact that, the moment the movement of their flesh stops and their music ceases, all that follows is the absolute white noise of the end. Moving on, creating realities, truly is within adventure, a matter of life or death.

But the sound produced by movement is not the only one that exists within adventure. Also present, although more rarely, is the cracking sound of bones crashing in battle. When confronted with the external powers of dominant abstractions – always ravenous, as they are, for more prey – adventurers might sometimes decide to engage in open confrontation. Once again, such sounds of war exist against a starkly unmusical background. Differently from the Just Wars waged by the armies obedient to dominant abstractions – carried out on the sound of morally reassuring, historically motivated chants – adventurers have to build their relationship with violence on the grounds of an absolute ethical responsibility. No superior moral codes or official courts will absolve them from their actions. No justice ever infuses their deeds. Only the struggle between empathy and desire – or, indeed, their harmony – can help them decide which level of violence is acceptable or which actions can be justified. Adventurers are heroes whose only narrators are themselves.

Indeed, adventurers' active creation of the world they inhabit is inextricably connected to their feelings of empathy. If through the creation of their surrounding landscapes – or, more precisely, dreamscapes – adventurers expanded their potency to the point of including parts of reality within their existential world, then through empathy they also include such reality within their emotional and affective territory. We could also describe this as a form of responsibility: once adventurers create the world they live in, they are also destined to feel for it, that is, to feel its resonance with themselves. As interactions progress and one's world expands, including a growing number of others – friends, enemies or strangers that they may be – such resonance also expands, putting itself at the core of one's ethical reasoning. Happy orphans of the moral codes of dominant abstractions, adventurers have no celestial table of laws to look at in their dealings with others; only the feeling of their resonance with them. As the experience of sex shows us, this is possibly the safest road to mutual pleasure, as opposed to the deadly paths laid down by the divine commandments of Work and History.

Maps

At last, even bones dissolve.

Like the pristine whiteness of revealed bones, every adventure terminates with a happy ending. We must be clear: the word 'happy' shouldn't lead us to think of a particularly joyous outcome. Quite the contrary, as the ending of the adventure is the end of the adventurer's life. How can death be happy? The happiness of death is that of a happy solution, more than that of a happy moment. The happiness to which we refer thus resembles the Latin word *felicitas*, which, as well as to the flow of serotonin that comes with a happy occurrence, also refers to the felicitous, successful solution of an issue. In our case, the felicitous realisation of the adventure. Differently from happy endings in films or books, which only take place at the end of the sequence of events, this happy ending runs alongside every moment of the adventure as its hidden potential. Because of the very egoism that infuses it, life within adventure is a state of perennial readiness to meet its happy ending. To the violence of death, adventure opposes the calm of a constant, active, non-resentful ripeness. A happy death is what drops ripe fruit off a branch – never too late, never too soon. It is a seal, not a guillotine.

This readiness marks the triumph of adventurers over the paralysing embrace of fear. As opposed to the regime of dominant abstractions, in which people's frantic activity is mainly that of anxiously delaying meeting their end, adventure offers its protagonists a liberation from the fear of this final encounter.

What is left of the adventurers, after the end of their adventure?

Nothing, we might think, as we see their bones turning into dust under the grinding of time. Yet, if we look closer, if we make ourselves so minuscule to be able to sneak through the web of tunnels that open inside rocks, we will find that after all, something remains. As the skeleton dissolves, what remains is its fossil.

The fossil of adventure, differently from that of a cretaceous shell, is not the involuntary result of a corpse trapped within geology. Similarly to the language of burials, adventurers leave behind themselves a silent map of their journey. They do without the reassuring stockpiling of paraphernalia of the ancient tombs, and behind themselves they only leave the immaterial trace of an existential language. A map, in other words, made by the intricate web of their sailing wake.

As they prepare themselves to meet their happy ending, adventurers make sure to render the trace of their journey as understandable as possible for all those who, in the future, will happen to seek or stumble upon it. Thus, writing, in the widest possible sense, is as much a part of adventure as it is the movement through it.

This propensity for writing, which doesn't come without dangers, originates from two main sets of reasons. On the one hand, despite their continuous struggle against the spectres of immortality as offered by dominant abstractions, adventurers, like all humans, find it hard to resist the chimera of a life after their biological life. They understand that immortality is precluded to them, yet somehow they can't stop desiring it. Thus, writing – that is, putting the trace of their life into the immortal coffer *par excellence*, written language – can be for them a safe compromise between the desire for immortality as expressed by one of their inner populations, and the 'State reason' of their atheistic inner Civilisation.

On the other hand, adventurers can't but acknowledge the shared nature of their experience. Their constant resonance with those with whom they shared it, makes them equally resound – maybe only as if in a dream – with all those that will venture along similar trajectories after them. If there is one chance for the love of adventurers to expand outside the boundaries of their flesh, it is possibly only through writing that such love for comrades they never met can take place.

Yet, adventurers remain aware that by leaving behind an abstract trace of their existential journey, they are also leaving a dangerous legacy. From then on, it will be the responsibility of future adventurers to handle such legacy carefully, possibly even with suspicion. But also, exactly by doing so, it might well be that those future adventurers will start their quest for their own adventure.

Vanishing

Throughout this book, adventurers have been described using an array of traditionally insulting denominations: radical atheists, squanderers, disrespectful opportunists, egoists, hypocrites, parasites. A list which seems to be taken out of right-wing tabloids, as they present the social monster of the day to their credulous readers.

Admittedly, choosing shocking words to define oneself is in no way an original idea. From the early Christians – who used to rename themselves self-demeaningly, with names such as Paulus, 'Little One', or with the early general common denomination Ebionites 'the poor ones' – to 20th Century Cubists, who employed an insult as the name for their movement, to 'nigga' hip hop artists, and so on, a great number of marginalised groups have often opted for such negative narcissism. Most of them decided to wear their chosen insult as a shining uniform, thus turning their social invisibility into the most visible of all flags. Paradoxically, by stating their irreducible difference with the surrounding cultural and social environment, they advocated for themselves a visible place within it. Apart perhaps from the early Christians – who were compelled to secrecy by persecution – they all employed their negative definition to such an extent, that eventually it became part of accepted common parlance.

Adventurers are different. Their squandering and disrespectful opportunism are in no way aimed at begging any legitimacy within the society they live in. They have no majoritarian ambition, nor any desire to be recognised as a respectable minority within society. Similarly to early Christians, their life-practice is the object of a fierce social persecution. Differently from them, however, their persecution cannot be redeemed by any seizure of power. Adventurers are antisocial by definition, in that they refuse to recognise Society as a legitimate abstract entity to which they could swear allegiance. While early Christians mitigated their social invisibility with the belief of an eternal visibility within their God's heavenly kingdom, adventurers hold no such hope. Not only do they not believe in the possibility of ever making their existential condition visible, in this life or in an imagined heaven to come, but they hold no desire whatsoever for this to happen. Social recognition only applies to social fictions, while one's existential choices need the darkness of social oblivion in order to grow fully.

Adventurers' desire for social obscurity informs their practices, as well as their personal aesthetics. Adventurers must be invisible, unrecognisable, as if living in hiding. To a social environment that demands the full visual expression of oneself as a tribute that one has to pay to the ghost of Freedom, they respond with a form of visual asceticism. To a society that imposes the diktat of appearing, they respond with a strategy of vanishing.

If the radical atheism, squandering and disrespectful opportunism of a life of adventure is considered immoral – if not outright illegal – then vanishing is the most effective mode of existence. And what better vanishing is there, within a landscape of dissimulated conformism, than the full embrace of the most banal visual conformity? With the same attitude of thieves and spies, adventurers swap the temptation of wearing a uniform of their own, with the advantages of disappearing in the darkness of visual social uniformity. Adventurers look boring, because boredom is the darkest of all possible clothes.

Invisible to all, adventurers are also invisible to each other. 'Unions of egoists' will be hard to develop, as the sum of the vanishings of their members only results in increased darkness, thus reducing its potential for attraction. Their proliferation on a large scale is nearly impossible. But the tasks they are set up for don't require multitudes of people. The number of those who will happen to find each other, like burglars accidentally meeting in front of the same house at night, or explorers stumbling on each other's maps, will suffice. Even when engaging in warfare, adventurers rely on strategies of small numbers. Theirs is asymmetrical warring, only aimed towards pleasure, sabotage or looting – never towards the ambition of founding empires or seeking mass martyrdom.

For all the rest, for the great conquests and the total wars, other means might be more appropriate. Outside of the 'union of egoists', there is politics.

Postscript

The Politics of Adventure in Real Life

Politics

Originally this short book was to be titled 'The Politics of Adventure'. But it didn't take me long to realise that this is a book on ethics and (to a lesser extent) war, not a book on politics. True, there were traces of so-called micro-politics in it, like those that take place within a group of friends or comrades, or between one's personal life experience and one's immediate environment. But the very definition of politics as applied to such processes never managed to convince me.

In the last few decades, especially on the left, there has been a trend towards an abnormal expansion of the field of politics. Today, politics seems to stretch to the point of encompassing just about everything – resembling theology at the height of the Middle Ages. According to the Egyptian feminist writer Nawal el Saadawi, for example, 'the moment there are two people in a room, there is politics'. I believe such an abnormal swelling of the field of politics is not only arbitrary, but is also detrimental to politics itself, as well as to the life of individuals.

If I had to provide a definition, I would say that politics has to do with the relationship between a collectivity and the available and necessary resources, with the aim of employing such resources to increase the happiness of the collectivity – if we understand collectivity as the sum of its individual members, and happiness as a perception which can only belong to individuals as individuals.

In other words, politics is an evolution of economic science – which simply deals with the relationship between people and resources – through the introduction of the finality of happiness, and of the boundaries of an individually-constituted collectivity.

The moment the field of politics is stretched to include and regulate the relationships between people, the result is the economisation of the human: individuals are reduced to the status of mere resources. They are then considered as dispensable, replaceable, in need of being employed for a 'superior' and external purpose. Once this happens, the way is open to the implementation of repressive and totalitarian structures.

There is politics, there is camaraderie, and there is war. And it is important to keep the three things separated.

Myth of the Origin

Let us take one step back. In order to clarify what stated above, let us begin with the very origin of our definition of politics.

Any political consideration rests on some type of 'myth of the origin'. Not the origin of the world – although also that myth is slowly making its way through posthuman disciplines – but the origin of Society. The most common version of this myth, which finds its most famous advocate in Hobbes, can be roughly summed up like this: "Once upon a time, humans lived in the state of nature, and spent their time hurting and killing each other. Until one day – maybe out of sudden enlightenment, progressive exhaustion or the arrival of a political messiah – they decided to stop their murderous habits and to unite in Society."

In a departure from such a myth, politics and political science has progressively evolved along a path that sees struggle, conflict and war not only as dominant parts of political life, but as the (negative) reason for the very existence of the political.

According to this view, humans are the main threat to human life, and human violence is both the illness and the cure around which politics revolve. The result of this perspective, which is truly transversal to the political fields of left and right, has been the focusing of political discourses on issues of conflict, domination and power.

I would like to claim that such a myth of the origin is not the only possible one. I believe that such view misunderstands the possibilities of politics, that it is detrimental to human life and that it attempts to include within the field of politics elements that can find better explanations through other conceptual tools.

Let us begin, in accordance to tradition, with our alternative version of the myth of origins. Instead of starting with "once upon a time" however, we will try to do without any fictional historicisation of the origin of Society. Instead, we will locate our question on the origin of Society in the very present time in which we live. Our question, then, is no longer "why *did* people decide to live in Society?", but rather "why *do* we live in society?"

Not Out of Love

The most immediate answer to our question, and the most obvious one, is that we were born in a Society. Despite the innermost wishes of some contemporary primitivists, we are already thrown since birth into a hyper-complex and seemingly all-encompassing social landscape. However, this answer cannot be enough to satisfy our question. Many are the things that we are born into, but their pre-existence is hardly a motivation for our supine acceptance of them. We can thus refine our question by rephrasing it as "why do we *accept* to live in Society?"

The tone of this new question clearly reveals a character of social life of which we are all well aware: life within Society is not only an imposition over us, but also an unpleasant one. Especially over the last century, human conglomerates have reached a volume and a level of interconnectivity that is light-years away from small societies such as ancient Athens, where the fundamental tools and concepts of politics first originated. We live in the age of megalopolises, tower blocks, crowded underground trains, queues, urban alienation, global wars, and so on. Society, at times, seems to resemble an overpopulated, alienating prison.

We can thus begin to answer our question by stating that we do not accept to live in Society because social life is innately good. We can also add that we do not live in Society out of love for our fellow humans: it is only a tiny minority of members of our Society whom we personally know, against a monumental background of virtually faceless people. Searching for an answer to our question, and keeping in mind the costs of life in Society, we will thus have to look for benefits that will be able to counterbalance such costs. What is at stake here is not just the lazy exercise of easy philosophising, but the realisation of whether Society is or can ever be more than a crippling factor for humanity. The pressing question that really lurks behind the facade of our seemingly theoretical issue is, "should we accept to live in Society, or should we rather try to escape from it altogether?"

Indeed, Society does not only come with costs, but also with benefits. We could state, finally answering our original questions (though still very vaguely), that the benefits of life in Society are the reasons for our acceptance of it. But what are those benefits?

If we had asked such a question to those living during pre-Roman antiquity or during the Middle Ages, their answer would probably have either concerned the practical necessities of agricultural labour, or the need to fulfill obscure religious commandments. In either case, the type of Society that they would have required could have easily coincided with the narrow boundaries of a contemporary kibbutz or of an anarchist commune. Asking such question today, however, leads us to completely different scenarios.

A Moral Imperative for Society

Unless we desire to return to the delights of life in the Middle Ages – with abysmal life expectancy, very poor health, very limited access to different types of food, etc – we can safely say that we are now accustomed to the benefits of a technically advanced, industrial Society. Advanced healthcare, food diversity, insulated homes, running water, the internet, digital libraries, high-speed transport and so on, can only be achieved through an industrial and gigantic Society such as the one we live in.

If as we said, the benefits provided by Society are our reasons for accepting it, then we can state that the specific benefits we just enumerated – and many other similar benefits which we didn't mention – constitute the reason for our acceptance of living in contemporary Society. We could proceed by claiming that, since these are the reasons that justify the existence of Society, then they must constitute the 'good' towards which Society should strive. Speaking in ethical terms, the identification of the 'good' leads to the possibility of building a set of moral norms. However, differently from what we are used to – that is, the imposition of moral norms upon us, by the hand of Society – this time it is us, the members of Society, who can impose moral norms upon it. Thus, when we talk about the provision of such benefits, we are stating the moral task of Society and we are declaring the criterion to value Society's success or failure.

In this sense, it is not only the theoretical availability of the benefits, but their *actual* and *universal* – as universal as our globalized Society is – availability which constitutes the practical implementation of Society's own morality. The universal availability of free and public healthcare, free and public transportation, free and public food supplies, free and public energy, free and public housing, free and public education, free and public knowledge, and so on, is not just one of the possible directions towards which Society might want to progress – as certain politicians claim – but it is *the only possible moral imperative for Society.*

The *universal availability of free and public services* is thus the reason for our acceptance of living within Society, or, more darkly, it is the criteria which separates a willful existence within Society from the annihilating subjection to a social megamachine. From this, we can derive how politics – understood as the science and art of putting Society to use – has essentially and exclusively to do with finding ways for such free and public services to be universally available. As a corollary, and in passing, we can also note how neoliberal policies aimed at cutting or privatising the Welfare state are not simply one of the various, legitimate political directions, but are a betrayal of politics as such, a misunderstanding of the function of Society and a dangerous, heart-chilling attempt at transforming Society into a planetary prison-industrial complex.

Warfare

But then what about conflict? If politics is only concerned with the common effort of making free and public services universally available, what place is left for what we used to define as 'political' struggle? As I claimed at the beginning of this postscript, there is another place, and another definition, which can host conflict more comfortably than the field of politics. This definition is 'warfare', and the place is the battlefield.

Politics has no room for conflict, power or domination, because politics is not a field of conflicting interests. Politics has one aim and one only – the universal provision of free and public services – and the only divergences that it may accept are those of different imaginations or technical opinions on how this could be best achieved. Conflict has to do with a completely different set of reasons, which can only be defined as pre-political. We might want to enter the battlefield in order to defy resistance and to make politics possible – yet, we cannot describe such conflict as political. This distinction between war and politics is not only a terminological issue, but also a deep conceptual difference that carries equally fundamental consequences.

Warfare, in its most technical and obvious sense, is a field in which the only legitimate aim is victory. Warfare is not a place for demonstrations, representation, polite discussion. The battlefield is not a ground for dancing opinions, liberal meekness, Christian self-flagellation. The battlefield is a ground that is starkly divided between victory and defeat – and nothing else.

Seen in this light, the political strategies of the contemporary Left in the West suddenly take a different colour. In the face of a State which daily misunderstands its moral role, turning Society into the nightmare of an overcrowded prison, and which protects its wrong-doings with a thick layer of warfare, the Left – and its ultra-left or anarchist neighbors – have recently responded with the pathetic deployment of self-defeating 'political' strategies. If the entrance to politics is defended militarily by a rogue State, it is necessary to acknowledge that our path towards politics has to pass through the battlefield of war. Demonstrations with raised hands, petitions, even the representational pantomime of the black bloc are of no use. Police brutality, mass imprisonments and repression are obvious responses from a State that seems more confident in understanding the rules of war than those of politics. Once again, the battlefield is a ground that should only be entered with the aim of winning, not with the smug desire to simply 'make a point'.

Warfare is a place of rational ruthlessness. Any means, any alliance is allowed, as long as it leads to long-lasting victory. Clearly, war is not only fought with guns and rockets, and different aspects of warfare have to be taken into account. Aside from a military strategy – which for too long the Left has cowardly dismissed – a strategy of wide alliances is necessary. Parliamentary opposition – as long as it is understood primarily as part of a war strategy – is as necessary as an infiltration within the armed forces, occupation of mainstream media is as funda-mental in our path towards victory as it is the continuous improvement of our tactics of sabotage.

If the path to politics is blocked, we must remove the garbage that is in our way. If our position is that of the defeated, we must strive towards victory. It would be a good start, if we began by restraining ourselves from the cowardly habit of disguising our failing warfare as hyper-complex politics. What is at stake is not the moral ground of our intellectual narcissism, but the possi-bility of forcing Society, maybe for the first time, to perform its moral duty.

Adventurers and The Left

How does this short book fit within this vision of war and politics? What are adventures and parasites to do?

Radical atheism, squandering and disrespectful opportunism are

ethical modalities of subjectivation – that is, of how one understands him or herself as a subject and an agent in the world –
which require alongside them the presence of a number of
external structures and services in order to truly, fully blossom.
Those structures and services – such as those mentioned above –
are the skeleton and function of politics.

It is for this reason that adventurers, radical atheists, squanderers, disrespectful opportunists or whatever we might want to
call them, could find it extremely important to join forces with
others – with whom they wouldn't necessarily share similar
existential trajectories – on the battlefield that separates them
from politics. Perhaps surprisingly, such an egoistic and inter-
ested alliance would have to include not only the most obvious
neighbours of the egoist individualist anarchism which animates
our vision of adventure – such as anarcho-syndicalists and auton-
omists – but also seemingly distant positions such as those
typically associated with the mainstream, parliamentary Left.

By any means, such alliances are only dictated by utility and
under no circumstances become a binding contract of loyalty.
Adventurers will always be disloyal, hypocritical allies. Any time
that their utility will be available through other means – legal or
illegal – the said alliance will be 'temporarily suspended' and
new paths will be explored. As discussed in the book, the
position taken by adventurers towards any institutional
counterpart is always that of the parasite: allied as long as the
host body provides them with nourishment, indifferent or even
hostile as soon as the host stops being useful.

For the time being however, and in consideration of the current
state of war, it would be convenient for anybody who wishes to
assume a radical atheist position join forces with those Left-
wingers who can effectively and realistically achieve victory on

the battlefield that stretches before politics. Although adventurers and mainstream Left-wingers might never become friends, they should gather on the same side of the barricade, possibly in intimate proximity. After all, a parasite needs to keep its host's body as close as it can.

Afterword

by Saul Newman

In 1844, in *The Ego and Its Own*, Max Stirner declared, 'Man your head is haunted... your head is haunted... You imagine great things, and depict to yourself a whole world of gods that has an existence for you, a spirit-realm to which you suppose yourself to be called, an ideal that beckons to you.' In his devastating critique of Feuerbach, Stirner unmasked the hidden religiosity lurking behind the edifice of secular humanism and its political form, liberalism. The figure of Man was simply God reinvented, another Christianised abstraction, another alienating spook, another altar on which the individual is sacrificed, this time in the name of the cruellest and most unforgiving god of all, his own Essence. And even Stirner could not have imagined the bloody sacrifices that would follow, sacrifices performed in the name of some Ideal or other – Humanity, Nation, Race, Socialism, Democracy. Stirner always warned us about the danger of Causes and their tendency to immolate to them all that is real, unique and sensuously alive in the individual.

Some might say that surely our times today have outlived the great Causes of modernity; that in our nihilistic, post-ideological age we no longer believe in anything, let alone be prepared to sacrifice ourselves and our enjoyment for any ideal. Yet, as Federico Campagna shows, we believe like never before. We are religious through and through. Our churchly vestments are our work clothes we put on every morning; our rites and liturgies, obsessively and piously performed, are our daily travails of work and consumption. Our faith is our belief on a return on our investment, our reward for a life of drudgery; our martyrdom is the suffering, humiliation and despair that comes with a wasted life. Campagna says that a life of work, of frenetic activity and feverish self-abnegation in the hope of some eternal reward, is simply bad investment. The icy waters of egotistical calculation that Marx thought characterised capitalism and drowned out religious fervour, are themselves immersed in the murkier depths of obscure and improbable beliefs, and our cost-benefit analyses are really the miserable scales in which we trade our lives and enjoyment for the most unreal and intangible of idols, our future salvation in the mystical kingdom of profit and loss. As Stirner would say, our times are literally alive with the spectres and abstractions of religious idealism, and that a ghostly apparition, an 'indwelling spirit', travels within us, just as we, like ghosts, travel to and from our places of work.

Campagna has written nothing less than a new, updated *Ego and Its Own* for our contemporary neoliberal age – an age in which the individual ego supposedly reigns supreme and unfettered, yet where, in reality, the individual is smothered by the heavenly ecstasies of belief and self-renunciation. La Boëtie's voice can be heard here too: the 16th Century theorist of voluntary servitude, who expressed astonishment at our willing submission to the power, which was after all only illusory, of tyrannical monarchs, he would be even more surprised at the way we freely cut our own throats and submit daily to a financial and economic tyranny which is no longer even clothed in symbolic power and authority. Perhaps the sadness of our times lies in the fact that there is no longer any figure of power which can serve as an excuse for our voluntary servitude, that the mechanism of our submission is entirely visible to us, and that – perhaps for this very reason – we submit now more than ever.

Enough of supplication! Enough of the wretched rags of our existence today; enough of our monk's habit and beggar's clothes, of the sackcloth and ashes in which we perform our daily penitence! It is time that, as La Boëtie urges, we recall to ourselves our own power and put a stop to this continual giving up of ourselves. It is time that, in Stirner's words, we become egoists. Campagna refers here to squandering as a practice of radical atheism – we should stop saving up for the afterlife and become, instead, spendthrifts of ourselves. It is not a question of chasing after some abstract spook like Freedom, a reheated dish served up to us by vanguards, now lukewarm. It is rather the assertion of an ontological freedom - a recognition that we are *always already free*. To see the world through egoistic eyes is to refuse the renunciation of the self and its enjoyment. It is not a question of atomistic, selfish individualism or the war of all against all; to associate egoism with the neoliberal model is, as we have said, to ignore the piety, veneration and loss of self that underpins it. Egoism means, on the contrary, that we can love one another in new ways; egoism is the basis for new and more intense forms of comradeship and togetherness that do not, at the same time, involve the sacrifice of the individual to the collective. Stirner talks about the 'union of egoists' – a seemingly paradoxical formulation, but one that, I believe, opens up a new space for thinking about both ethics and politics. In the same vein, Campagna talks about the comradeship of adventurers.

To embark on adventures, individually and in cooperation with others, is to turn one's life into an adventure, to open up lines of flight. It is to affirm the contingency of one's existence, and to chart new paths of escape. Like the May '68 insurgents used to say, it is to find the beach beneath the paving stones (*Sous les pavés, la plage*). Above all, it involves an ethical mode of life – not an existence crushed under the weight of moral abstractions and self-laceration, but on the contrary, an ethics of both autonomy and joyous companionship. It also serves as a reminder to be on our guard against Causes, even – and especially – revolutionary ones, for what could these be other than a new demand for sacrifice. Stirner talked about 'possessedness': we can be possessed by many things, by all sorts of spooks and abstractions – God, Man, Morality, the State, Property – but also, at times, by our own desires and passions, which, if they take over our lives, become no different from other idols and lead to the same sort of religious devotion and self-sacrifice. Stirner referred to this as a 'one-sided, unopened, narrow egoism'. Campagna seeks to avoid the same trap, and the notion of adventure, rather than narrow, enclosed and self-seeking, is an opening out of the self onto the world. Squandering is neither the realisation of some underlying essence, nor the securing of an identity; it is the deterritorialising of all fixed identities and the creation of something new.

Like Stirner before him, Campagna has written something novel, singular and dangerous. Not a prayer book for ideologues, but something between an ethical meditation and Molotov cocktail that can be thrown against the abstractions that imprison us.

zero
books

Contemporary culture has eliminated both the concept of the public and the figure of the intellectual. Former public spaces – both physical and cultural – are now either derelict or colonized by advertising. A cretinous anti-intellectualism presides, cheerled by expensively educated hacks in the pay of multinational corporations who reassure their bored readers that there is no need to rouse themselves from their interpassive stupor. The informal censorship internalized and propagated by the cultural workers of late capitalism generates a banal conformity that the propaganda chiefs of Stalinism could only ever have dreamt of imposing. Zer0 Books knows that another kind of discourse – intellectual without being academic, popular without being populist – is not only possible: it is already flourishing, in the regions beyond the striplit malls of so-called mass media and the neurotically bureaucratic halls of the academy. Zer0 is committed to the idea of publishing as a making public of the intellectual. It is convinced that in the unthinking, blandly consensual culture in which we live, critical and engaged theoretical reflection is more important than ever before.